Praise for *Manifestation Magic*

"Elhoim shares a beautiful, compelling perspective on manifestation magic rooted in his personal practice, diverse studies, and experience growing up in a magical family in Venezuela. His poetic style will inspire and provide a vivid and welcome complement to the host of useful, practical information contained here. *Manifestation Magic* is a wonderful contribution to the field of practical magic." –Durgadas Allon Duriel, author of *The Little Work*

"Leafar's passion is conveyed abundantly in *Man~~~~~~~ ~~~~~ ~~ ~~~ ~~~* cessful teaching style. As an initiate of the Art brings to light a unique, powerful blend of s wealth. Using visualization, candle magic, cryst guides readers into the realm of manifesting the of *Horse Magick* and *Dragonflame*

T0046346

"Get ready to manifest your best life with Elhoim Leafar's latest offering: *Manifestation Magic*. Leafar is a beaming light of positivity in the magical community and this comprehensive book is his torch for guiding others on their path. With a diverse and expansive approach to spellcasting and ritual, this book speaks to the modern magic makers of today–showcasing the potently powerful means for tapping into the endless enchantment of the universe. I highly recommend this book for anyone looking to bewitch their lives with an abundance of magic!" –Michael Herkes, author of *The GLAM Witch* and *The Complete Book of Moon Spells*

"Leafar has poured his heart and soul into *Manifestation Magic*. His pages are filled with unique perspectives from his experiences of magic as an urban shaman. This book is an intimate look into the practices of a magician who hails from Venezuela." –Najah Lightfoot, author of *Good Juju*

"Written by a master of the metaphysical, *Manifestation Magic* is a remarkable and comprehensive guide to realizing one's utmost desires of fruitfulness. In a tone that made me feel as if Elhoim Leafar was at my side teaching me, he explains not only how to clear oneself of both the observable and unobservable obstacles preventing success but also how to effectively do so without sustaining any feelings of guilt or reservations about the stigmas associated with prosperity. In step-by-step fashion, readers learn about the candles, crystals, and entities, as well as the lunar, solar, and planetary energies that aid in manifesting abundance. The rituals are unique, and the suggested spells are outstanding. Once again, I have been left enraptured by the unparalleled brilliance of Leafar." —Miss Aida, author of *Hoodoo Cleansing and Protection Magic*

"Elhoim is among those we call 'wise ones'—special souls who are highly attuned to the magic that exists all around us. His book *Manifestation Magic* is a huge download of profound magical wisdom that will shock you into knowing your own power, while gently and simply teaching you how to transform your existence step-by-step. Beginner magicians will feel supported, as they begin their journey into magic, while experienced practitioners will be blown away by Leafar's profound insights. I refer to this book often and recommend it to anyone who wants to truly master the art of manifestation." —Madame Pamita, author of *Madame Pamita's Magical Tarot* and *The Book of Candle Magic*

"*Manifestation Magic* is a thorough, yet approachable guide, suitable for beginners. Its exercises are refreshingly new and exciting, while Leafar's insights are always interesting. This is a great addition to any magickal library." —Lilith Dorsey, author of *Orishas, Goddesses, and Voodoo Queens*

"True wisdom and knowledge are written within the pages of *Manifestation Magic*. Whether you are a beginner or have been practicing for years, you will get something from this book, or it will remind you of something that you've forgotten about working with abundance. In this easy read, the exercises are simple but powerful. This is a must-have for any practitioner's library." —Amanda Keith and TJ Vancil, owners of 3 Crows Conjure and Occult Master Class

"*Manifestation Magic* is bursting with foundational knowledge for magical crafting, along with invaluable wisdom on the nature of courting the spirits of abundance in your life for long-lasting success. You'll discover a full spectrum of magical practices that are rooted in tradition and years of personal practice. Leafar truly displays the empowering qualities of magic as an art and way of life." —Shaheen Miro, author of *Lunar Alchemy* and *The Uncommon Tarot*

Manifestation Magic

21 Rituals, Spells, and Amulets
for Abundance, Prosperity, and Wealth

Elhoim Leafar

WEISER
BOOKS

This edition first published in 2021 by Weiser Books, an imprint of
Red Wheel/Weiser, LLC
With offices at:
65 Parker Street, Suite 7
Newburyport, MA 01950
www.redwheelweiser.com

ISBN: 978-1-57863-742-3
Library of Congress Cataloging-in-Publication Data available upon request.

Cover design by Kathryn Sky-Peck
Cover art © Soft Muse Art
Interior illustrations by David F. Dagnino Viloria
Interior by Ellen Varitimos
Typeset in Avenir

Printed in the United States of America
IBI
10 9 8 7 6 5 4 3 2 1

"That person, male or female, who wants to dedicate his spirit to the 'Magical Arts' must possess a true vocation for it, putting all his will and good faith in his exercises and practices."
—Jonas Sufurino, *The Book of St. Cyprian*

To all those who have thought that they are looking for magic in their lives, without realizing that it is magic that is looking for them.

To all those who have perceived that call, which goes beyond borders, colors, and languages.

To all those who have found an alliance in magic, and yet continue to learn in the constant process.

To all of you, and to all those who will learn from you.

Contents

PART II: ABUNDANCE, PROSPERITY, AND WEALTH

PART III: DESIRES, WISHES, AND SPELLS

PREFACE

September 27, 2015. Lacking any knowledge of English beyond a simple "Hello. How are you?" or "Bye, bye, bye," I got off the plane in Atlanta and proceeded to search for my connecting flight to New York City. I carried a suitcase with my old laptop, a Kindle, my grimoire, many books, six charm bags, two changes of clothes, my toothbrush, and fifteen dollars. I knew practically no one, and clearly nobody knew me. I didn't have a job lined up or the name of a lawyer, much less any money to pay one. Five months later, I was signing a publishing contract with a large publishing house, while working full-time doing readings during weekends. Now, four years later, I am writing this book to teach you how I did it from scratch, what I had to learn, and what I learned to do.

A WORD TO READERS– OUR GODS AND ANGELS

In this book the gods of good fortune and prosperity are mentioned constantly, that is just my perspective on the matter, a perspective that comes from my background, my personal and family heritage, my daily practice, and my origin. Many believe in angels and faeries, and in a way I do, too. I see angels as the divine manifestations as they really are: messengers.

If you believe in angels, and they are part of your daily personal practice, I invite you to read this book and interpret my *gods of good fortune* as the angels of light and joy that illuminate your path.

This book was written with enormous and infinite love, and it was written for you. You have the power to interpret it in whatever way makes you happy. The intention and purpose of this book are to help you achieve happiness, economic prosperity, and abundance. Do not seek to become a millionaire, seek to become prosperous, with your happiness as the ultimate goal. If it makes you happy to see these gods as angels or vice versa, I invite you to do so freely.

Religions, groups of believers, spiritual tribes, and covens, they are all branches of that immense tree that we are all climbing to reach the sunlight at the top.

Gods, angels, and faeries are all divine manifestations of the nature of the universe, just as you are.

Blessed be today and forever.

PART ONE

Magic and Sorcery

The mistake that many of us make is to believe that we have come here to get comfortable, when the truth is that we have come here to get uncomfortable, to learn and evolve in the process. And the study and practice of magic is a reminder of that.

1

Magic

Be conscious, don't forget to be aware of the magic you do, the rituals you craft, and the power you have. Incredible powers embrace every cell in your body, don't let any situation, emotion, or person make you think otherwise.

Philosophy and *Esoteric Study* are terms that try to give you a hundred different ideas about what magic really is and how it is used. In this book I am not trying to evangelize anyone. I am not going to proclaim that this is the only valid concept, and I will not try to fill your head with such complex information. Although it may be correct, it will always be incomplete, because defining something as complex as magic is as difficult as questioning a group of philosophers about the origin of life and its function. We could spend a lifetime researching the origin of magic and its practice and still never reach a single conclusion.

Because of that, this book will begin with a short but essential journey toward the discovery of your power and the use of magic and sorcery for your own benefit. However, the most important part of this trip will not be to learn, but rather to unlearn. If this book came into your hands, you already have learned something about magic from other books, movies, a past life, or other personal experiences.

This book will not cover the origin of the word *magic* or its uses through the complicated history of humanity. What it will focus on are the simplest experiences without pretension—the energy you feel in your fingertips when your hands are underwater, the instinct that guides you to make certain decisions, even when everyone tells you its wrong, the first impulse of a pregnant mother as her baby's heart beats, the feeling of empathy with a stranger in the street, that *something* that tells you not to enter that alley or alerts you when someone is following you, the premonitory dreams you have at night. All these experiences with different names (intuition, premonition, instinct, empathy, telepathy, clairvoyance) are linked by a fine energetic bond that connects them to each other and, in turn, connects them with you. That fine bond is magic, and in its subtle touch are the greatest powers that govern and connect all the creative and transformative forces in this universe.

Wizards, sorcerers, witches, fortune-tellers, shamans, and alchemists all have their own definition of what magic is and many of them probably use it for different reasons—to attract love, earn more money, heal diseases, cure the evil eye, protect their home, predict the future, consider the past, and so forth. All of them share something in common—the mystical art of magic.

Although all the mystical processes of life are linked to each other by magic, these processes represent and are linked in turn to different types of energy—psychic, shamanic, mystical, spiritual, and so forth. Sorcery is, for many scholars, the field that studies these practices, and through sorcery in its different aspects you can learn to better channel these energies and make use of them for your own well-being.

For many theorists, sorcery includes a group of knowledge, practices, techniques, and tools for studying magic. I propose to use *the study of magic* for the theoretical, and *sorcery* to refer to the practical application of this knowledge.

Visualizing Magic

A moment of magic, like a deep feeling of healing, a tiny omen in the wind, a prayer from the mouth of a mother, a deep light in the horizon, is sometimes everything you need to awake your power.

Let's do a small visualization exercise together. Start by breathing deeply and slowly for a moment, looking carefully at all the beings and objects around you: people, animals, plants, electronic equipment, and so forth. Take your time with this visualization. If you want to make it shorter, count a number of objects, things, and people around you, there can be twelve, twenty, fifty, two hundred, or easily 5,800 different things.

Now visualize that your hands are covered by a thin, fine, bright, and translucent halo of light and assign a color to it, it can be white, yellow, orange, blue, any color that makes you feel good. (If choosing a color is hard, I suggest you visualize a bright and translucent white halo.) Now visualize this halo as thin as a sheet of paper, but still visible.

Now, imagine that the halo of bright light not only covers your hands, but rather your whole body, and while you visualize this, think about something very simple—that the halo that you are visualizing really exists. It is not something you imagined. It is not something new that you are creating, quite the opposite, it is something very old that you are just now discovering. That halo of light that covers you has always been there, only now you are giving it color and form to force it to manifest itself. Now that you understand that it has always been there, you will begin to notice that the visualization becomes easier, and you will also notice certain slight changes in that halo, such as its color and density.

Finally, we will return to the objects you counted and try to visualize them wrapped in that same halo of light that covers you, see for example a tree, your smartphone, a cup of coffee on the desk, even this book. Visualize all these objects covered by this halo of light, and, "Surprise!" it will not take long to notice that while you visualize these objects, a very thin line of bright, almost invisible light connects some part of your body with one of these objects or people.

Stay with this exercise for a few more minutes. Take a deep breath, eliminate any distraction from your head, and you will see that these lines of light that radiate off you are connected with absolutely everything around you, even things that are not yours, even things that are unknown, cars in the street, houses, briefcases, vases, a traffic light, a mountain. Once you have noticed these fine lines of light you will understand two very simple truths in life:

> The first thing you'll understand is that those halos of vaguely visible light that connect everything around you are magic. Give it another name if you prefer, but that is magic and it is in you and in all things. Through sorcery you will learn to handle those fine, thin lines to attract what you need and want.

> The second thing you will understand is as important as the first. It's that everything around you, absolutely everything, is connected, from the sky to the ground, and beyond, and once you understand this, the use of the magical arts will take on a much deeper meaning for you.

Magic and Energy

A force that governs everything from the beginning to the end.

Magic governs all, it is a force that has existed from the origin of everything and will continue to exist after all. It is an abundant and thriving force that will always instinctively try to connect, create, produce, reproduce, and transform everything it touches. It also tries to help them grow and prosper, from attracting good customers to a commercial space to attracting numerous burning stars to planetary systems larger than ours.

Visualize magic as a primal force, as a sun that does not stop burning, a star that does not stop shining, or a planet that does not stop spinning around a gravity well. Look at the moon at night, and remember that this moon is attracted by the gravitational force of the earth, while the earth is attracted by the gravitational force of the sun, and it in turn is being attracted by a much larger gravitational force. They all act as a result of some power. The Earth doesn't think, "I'm going to settle here to turn around the sun for a while until I get tired." The Moon doesn't think, "I was bored and went to visit Earth to give her some light at night." No, that does not happen, these elements move because something much larger than them attracts them, the force of gravity.

In the universe we inhabit, magic is not an exception to the rule, it is a supreme force that acts by instinct seeking to attract, multiply, and transform. Even karma, that divine force that rules over all living and thinking beings, has an important role in this matter, because magic acts as a messenger and transformer of karmic desires, for better or worse.

Mages for thousands of years (at least ten millennia if we consider druids, hierophants, and sorcerers of mankind's oldest pagan temples) have made in-depth use of this fine art of sorcery, together with alchemy, to be able to transform the entire environment that surrounds them, including governments, homes, families, models of thought, and even the weather.

This force that connects everything, magic itself, is extremely powerful and capable of giving you literally everything you need. That is why in this guide we focus on using your own energy and magical power to attract and transform your life and the lives around you for the better.

The Work Behind Your Rituals

How do they work, what do they consist of, and how do we perform them? All the work that was done before, step by step, chant by chant, that is where the magic happens.

If sorcery is the application of the magical arts and all the techniques and secrets that are hidden around it, a spell or ritual is a magical work carried out in a specific order to focus our energy on transforming a situation, thought, or anything else, into something different. Similar to a cooking recipe, a spell entails a series of elements, full attention on its realization, a lot of focus, time, and the desire to do it. And just like cooking in the kitchen, if you lose focus, the food will burn.

There are many attributes and elements involved in magic and sorcery: the hours of the day, the days of the month, your emotional state, and the magical tools you use. Even clothing and the environment can be important factors, especially for beginners, who may have a harder time focusing their energy and concentrating on what they are doing, because if you don't feel comfortable—if your shoes are too tight, you never liked that shirt, or the room is too cold—you will become completely distracted.

Performing a spell or ritual entails proper preparation, and it is important that you erase various concepts from your head—as mentioned above, it is time to unlearn. It is hard to fill your head with new knowledge if it is already full of information. For that reason, I recommend you use the scientific method as you study, meaning you must always assume that anything you learn today may become obsolete tomorrow, especially in a field as complex as metaphysics. So you must be prepared to study many different concepts from various authors and teachers. Once you put them into practice, you can decide which of them you have the strongest connection with and which methods work best for you.

To realize a spell, it is necessary to take into account the time when it will be performed. Some rituals and spells, including those involving the elements of fire, earth, and sun, the transformation of an individual's conscious mind, and the execution of creative energy for something new, usually become stronger when performed during the hours between dawn and a couple of hours before sunset, while rituals and talismans that involve the elements of water and air, the moon's energy, transformation of the unconscious, and the use of slower, more progressive transformational energy tend to have a faster, more powerful effect when performed at night, especially midnight (*the witching hour*).

Although the time of day to execute the ritual or spell is under the complete control of the sorcerer, the effective fulfillment of it has more to do with the desire requested, the energy used, the correct use of tools, the elements around the ritual, and many other factors. There are no exact times when it comes to magic. Although some rituals may take up to three months to complete, some may have rather immediate results. This will depend on many external and internal factors surrounding the sorcerer.

A sorcerer or mage with years of experience can perform a simple ritual to feel more energetic during the day and his spell can take effect in just one or two days, but a person with no experience, or who has only performed a couple of spells, did not concentrate properly during the ritual because he was distracted by his phone, or was unsure of the effects of the spell or not clear about his intentions, can perform exactly the same spell as the more experienced sorcerer, and it can take months to take effect. This might even make the performer doubt his results because they did not show up immediately.

Until you empty the glass, you cannot fill it again.

Until your head gets cleared of someone else's thoughts, there will be no room for new thoughts, experiences, learnings, and stories.

Learn to let go of old taboos and prejudices, in order to embrace new thoughts, new energies, new people, new places, learnings, and experiences.

2

SORCERY

---

*You do the **magic**, the **magic** will do the rest . . .*
And a little more.

If energy lives in different forms in absolutely everything that exists in our universe, and magic is the constant theoretical-practical study of the movement of this energy which leads us to understand its operation and movement (the influences of the phases of the moon or the power to charge amulets), sorcery is the set of techniques, practices, tools, and rituals that we carry out to realize that magical use, popularly known as *magical work* or *witchcraft*.

A spell is the ritual method used to identify the energy we are working with and to make use of it for our benefit or the benefit of others. If we use amulets, charm bags, potions, or symbols to attract and control some type of energy, we are using a spell, and the *spellcaster* or *sorcerer* acts as the mediator between the energy existing in a situation (the cause) and the result that it is being sought to produce (the effect).

The sorcerer as a mediator learns from theory and practice. Far from simply engaging in spells and rituals without a specific purpose beyond fulfilling a wish, for example, placing a love spell on someone because it is their desire to be loved by someone, the sorcerer focuses on studying the situation from the outside, understanding where the desire comes from (the origin), what result they are seeking to achieve with the ritual (the desire–to be loved), why they are using magic (accelerating the process and removing obstacles), and which magic method to use (a potion, enchantment, or invocation).

The true wisdom of the sorcerer is in his ability to identify what the problem is and what the options are to solve it, and for this, the sorcerer has to consult the guidance of his masters (teachers, spirits, ancestors, gods, Orixas), and thus determine what the appropriate method is for realizing his desire to resolve, improve, or change a situation—for better or worse.

The art of the sorcerer is found in the deepest and most complete understanding of serendipity, seeing forward to the events in a distant fate, accumulating all kinds of magical treasures and blessings, to influence each of these events for his own benefit or someone else's.

In this book, one of our goals is to help you become a sorcerer of your own pantheon, a connoisseur of your own magic, a guide to your own path, and a wise light that guides others who seek or meet you on that path.

Because of the above we will focus on a series of rituals for cleansing and purifying all those impediments that block your path to abundance, wealth, and well-being, using your own energy in combination with the power of your personal pantheon so that you can become a real light able to illuminate the path of others who follow.

Your Magical Skills

Your magic skills work like a muscle: if you want to show off your muscles or run a marathon faster, it won't help you to spend whole days sitting in front of the computer reading. No matter how much you learn about how to exercise your muscles, if you don't train each in the appropriate way, it is not going to grow stronger, and this can end up having serious effects on your health. Your ability to perform magic works exactly the same way: if you don't train your skills properly they will not develop and can instead be blocked.

You can read all the medical books in the library and take notes on each issue of a health care magazine but that does not make

*you a doctor; it only makes you a very good connoisseur of the
subject. Sorcery is no different.*

In magic and sorcery, practice is vitally important, and although
theory is also important, take into account that the wise druids, the
magicians and priests of the old European continent, and those first
witches of Salem did not exactly have a local library card or a bookstore
available. Although, yes, this was the time of obscurantism,[1] we cannot
deny that much of the magical knowledge we inherit comes from these
individuals whose practices were passed from generation to generation by oral tradition, who learned the correct use of herbs by collecting
them in the forest with their hands, and who conjured the spirits of the
night with candles, oils, a little blood, and some spells on parchment.
They learned by practicing, they had no time to read books, much less
enjoy the freedom to share them.

If you have not done any kind of spell consciously before, the
chances are that when you perform the rituals in this book you may feel
anxious, but that is a good sign that you want to do things right and you
are worried about the result. It means you are on the right track.

As your practice increases, you will begin to feel a greater sensitivity toward your own magic, toward your connection with the environment, and with other practitioners like you. Your connections with
nature, plants, and animals will become deeper and more intimate. You
will begin to see them with other eyes and even the perfume of the
rose will become more delicious to your nose. That is because, as your
abilities awaken, your connection with everything alive and natural in
your environment will have increased.

If at this step you continue performing the visualization exercise
I taught you at the beginning of the book, at least once a week, for
sessions of ten to fifteen minutes, you will notice that each of those

---

1   Obscurantism: An attitude contrary to the sharing of culture in society. Also, a historical period of
humanity where information remained restricted in its dissemination to the public, and only individuals
closest to the clergy of the dominant Church had access to manuscripts and books, as it was considered
inappropriate to grant this knowledge to ordinary people. The term *obscurantism* comes from the title
Epistolæ Obscurorum Virorum (Letters from the dark men) of a famous 16th century satire.

fine lines of light and subtle energy are more pronounced, firmer, with more color and brightness. You will feel that the energy moves to touch your skin, and you will even perceive in these fine halos of energy a multitude of colors that you did not notice before. After some time, you will even make this practice a form of conscious vision that will be activated unconsciously.

Now, if these skills for the practice of magic are not used, you might get numb to magic, what I like to call simply a blockage, which is similar to the sensation when you sit down to meditate, or assume the well-known Lotus Position, and your legs start to feel numb, the blood stops flowing well, and then you lose all sensation in them temporarily.

In magic this numbness is the same. If you don't use your magic, the energy stops flowing in and you get numb to it. Then that feeling of constant boredom, monotony, and tiredness invades you; in some cases you may even experience an inexplicable insomnia or excessive sleep. This is because if an ethereal muscle of your body might be charged with energy but is numb, the energy does not flow inward but also does not flow outward, and you feel like you are constantly carrying a heavy backpack that you do not remember picking up. It is simply there causing a nuisance, instead of being a useful tool.

Where Does Your Magic Come From?

The gods gathered at some time billions of years before the history of mankind and, through a long process, created the world we inhabit. They created the rivers and the seas, carved the mountains and forged each one of the thick groves, moved the waters of the world to different places to create the arid deserts, the splendid beaches, the deep lakes, and the islands and continents that would later be inhabited by the greatest of its creations, humanity.

Above all, our gods are our parents and creators, as well as teachers of a science much older than our understanding, which is why, like all parents, they gave us the tools to continue forging and transforming the work they created. We inherited the magic that remained on Earth, and through the sacred ancestral bonds that connect us with all our ancestors from within, we are able to access the profound wisdom of those ancient creator gods.

Once you wake up your bond with your ancestors, you will have access to a powerful energy that is capable of transforming absolutely everything that surrounds you. What separates the mages from non-mages is the understanding we have of that individual connection with everything that has preceded us. This sacred connection is powerful and infinite, and the more you explore it, the more power you can receive from it, because this connection with your ancestors works like elaborate wiring connecting you to the main battery—those gods of antiquity, the creators of everything.

While the connection of some magicians with their surroundings and their ancestors is powerful, some people have a more superficial and intermittent connection, but that connection is never limited. It will grow more and more with use. That connection is the reason why some individuals are born with certain special talents for the execution of the magical arts, while others discover them during a growth process, as an intuitive call to better understand the world.

Your abundance, like your craft, is a reflection of your inner magic, which is a reflection of your own understanding. Both are limitless, as are you. In a perfect universe, where time-space is constantly expanding and chaos ends up originating entire galaxies abundant in stars, each one of us as individuals is a reflection of this abundance; we are vibrant, changing beings, that are constantly expanding.

But just as the children of great musicians can also become great musicians but still remain in the shadow of of their parents, often it's those artists who don't descend from an outstanding family of musicians that turn out to be better known. Perhaps it's destiny or genetics, or simply because they work harder, because constant practice and daily study will always overcome (in results) innate talent. The secret to understanding your power is in your daily routine.

A Visualization Exercise

I recommend that you perform this meditation consistently but not daily. When I used to perform this exercise every week, the results took time to appear, but when I began to improve my visualization and my personal connection with this exercise, I was able to reduce it to once a month.

This meditation exercise gains additional strength and has better results if you do it between sunset and midnight on a new moon day.

To better understand the above concepts, sit in a comfortable position in a calm, quiet space at a time where you won't be interrupted, light your favorite flavor of incense to cleanse the space around you, then close your eyes, take several deep breaths, and feel the calm wash over you.

Visualize with your feet and your legs connected to the ground as roots. Visualize these roots growing down from your feet and piercing the ground, crossing the concrete, basements, and all the material world that separates you from Mother Earth. Do not visualize them as obstacles, but rather as small bridges that are there to connect you with the earth.

Imagine your roots growing and deepening into the earth. Breathe deeply and feel the temperature of the fresh earth your roots are entering, feel its texture and shape, visualize its color and the minerals and rocks that make up our planet.

You will begin to feel a slight itching in your feet, a warm tingling. Do not resist this sensation; instead, let yourself be carried away by it. It is the energy of your ancestors, of all those who preceded you and who now inhabit the earth beneath your feet—their bones, their skin, their ashes, each of their footsteps are in and on the earth.

Connect with Earth, feeling every beat of your heart rising through your roots. Feel these beats, calm your breathing, and slowly try to synchronize your heartbeat with her rhythms.

During this moment of sacred connection, you are becoming one with the land of your ancestors, ancestors who were different from you, embodied souls who dressed in other skins, other hair, other colors, and communicated in other languages. Those ancestors are numerous, and the more of them you visualize, the more of them you perceive, the more of them are connecting with you, beating with you, hugging your roots that were once their roots, and breathing with you.

You will begin to perceive a slight tingling in your ears. Do not scratch: it is the whisper of the voices of your ancestors reciting in your ears the prayers that they made to their first gods, to their first creators. Do not resist them, but embrace that tickle that walks through your skin, that knows you by your roots, and that slides under your skin.

Keep this connection for about ten more minutes, breathing deeply, and feeling the energy of your ancestors emerging from the earth and connecting with you through your roots. Keep connecting with them. Keep visualizing Earth's fleshy heart beating from the depths to you.

After the ten minutes are up, close the connection. If you try to keep the connection for longer, you may feel exhausted or fall asleep, because this exercise can easily drain you.

To close the connection you have created, take a deep breath and hold it for a few moments, then release the air. Repeat this breathing exercise. With each inhalation and exhalation, your roots become smaller reeling in toward you; feel how your roots come back and bring with them Earth's energy.

Once you have finished bringing up your roots and watching them transform back into your feet, thank those ancestors who have taken the moment to connect with you. Take one more deep breath and slowly open your eyes, get up carefully, and drink enough water to hydrate yourself.

Once you put this exercise into practice, you will understand a unique truth that has been denied you for a long time: This body that you have, your eyes, your face, your hair, your hands, even your skin and organs, all are just temporary. Your time in this world is temporary.

Your true existence is a sacred truth: you are the result of millennia of your ancestors' work. They live in you, and even when you die, regardless of whether you have offspring or not, your body and essence will return to the earth, your ashes will become part of the air mixed with the land of the mountains and the waters of the oceans, your essence will continue to evolve and grow, and after a time you will have the opportunity to incarnate again. But while that happens, you will be one of those many ancestors of humanity. If you are reading this book, it is because you are destined to understand that you will be a proud and powerful ancestor of the next generations.

Now that you understand this, it is important that you understand something else: that just as your physical body is nothing more than a temporary vessel for your essence, your body is also a *tool* of your essence, allowing it to mingle among the living, and among them, grow, learn, and evolve even more.

As a mage, you are destined to manifest in the physical world the power you can borrow from the spiritual and other worlds, including the magical power that comes from the earth, that essence remaining of the creator gods. And as every skilled, well-educated doctor knows, her greatest instruments are her hands, because they are the only way to make use of her tools and put into practice all the knowledge she possesses.

Your body is like that doctor's hands, and just like her, you are going to need a set of tools to carry out your magical operations. That is why in the next section I provide a complete list of the tools that every good mage must have to carry out proper practice.

With the use of these tools you can project, control, and manifest the energies in your environment, perform spells from the simplest rituals to the most powerful magic, and thus manifest your individual desires in the physical world.

Learn to flourish where you are, whatever the circumstances are.

Like the lotus, that blooms in the murky and stagnant waters,

Like the Goddess Lakshmi who stands firm on the lotus,

In order to cleanse and heal the world from the middle of rottenness.

The Tools of Sorcery

An old holistic science for everyone's understanding.

Tools are extremely important in sorcery. A magic tool is a functional and energetically charged object that is used to perform different types and classes of spells or to assist us in our rituals. The number of tools and their use can vary according to the needs of each practitioner. While some sorcerers can have a huge room dedicated exclusively to the storage of their tools, others opt for the simplicity of having the minimum necessary number of tools to perform their various spells and enchantments. Following is a list of these essential tools.

The Cup or the Chalice

A cup or chalice is an essential object on a magician's altar. Ideally it is made of metal or glass. It can also be made of different minerals such as amber or garnet, but never plastic.

It symbolizes the control of the water element in your hands. It is used to offer liquor and water to the spirits, as well as for divination works, as many magicians fill their glasses with dark wine to visualize auguries on its surface.

The cup should be be filled at all times to symbolize the water element and abundance. Keeping an empty cup in the sacred space of your altar is considered an omen of need and bad luck. Filling the glass with clear water every Monday night is a beautiful custom from the most modern spiritualist currents. You can also keep it filled with wine, honey, or fruit liquor to honor the spirits that are present in our environment, not just when we turn to them for favors and blessings.

In some Wiccan traditions the cup is also associated with femininity, fertility, and the Mother Goddess.

The Cauldron

The cauldron symbolizes the hardness and firmness of the earth, as well as its ability (as a planet) to contain all the elements and life itself.

The cauldron has been associated with magic and sorcery for centuries. You can find it in a wide variety of paintings and stories where it is usually accompanied by the image of an alchemist, a wizard, or a witch. It is the place where the spells of all practitioners are held. For the most modern magical traditions, it represents wisdom, with the cauldron acting as a skull, where all that is within it is pure, ethereal, and untouchable, like a metaphorical brain.

A cauldron filled with coarse salt keeps bad vibes away from the home, while a cauldron filled with dirt and stones symbolizes firmness. Certain beliefs of conventional voodoo recommend filling the cauldron with dirt from a local graveyard, ashes, and pulverized bones to conjure the grieving souls that have not achieved rest.

In my personal practice, and through my path of learning, I began to consider it a bad omen to keep your cauldron empty. It is a sign of scarcity and poverty, so I like to keep my cauldron (in addition to painted, decorated, and personalized), full of dried flowers and aromatic herbs, always near the altar, where it should remain as a source of prosperity and abundance.

The Censer

The censer is associated with the element of air which is often over-looked, but if you pay attention, the censer is always present in the space of a magician or sorcerer. It is well known that incense smoke not only dissipates evil, but also relaxes the mind and cleanses the environment. Seers make use of the smoke as a curtain that allows them to see between worlds and read auguries of the future.

The censer can be found in a variety of sizes, shapes, colors, materials, and presentations. You can find ceramic and marble censers with valuable decorative details and all kinds of magical symbols. My favorites are those made of bronze because they have longevity and are usually more popular, but wood ones are usually the most economical, easy to take anywhere, and you can even paint them to your liking.

A traditional spiritualistic practice teaches us to hold the censer with both hands while the smoke unfolds, blow the smoke in all directions of the room and then turn the whole body to the right to move the smoke around us. After five turns stop for a moment in complete silence and close your eyes for a few seconds. When you open them again, you can decipher all kinds of shapes and silhouettes in the smoke of the incense. These shapes in the smoke are announcements of destiny that are written in our environment, and through this simple ritual we can decipher them.

One of my daily mantras for more than fifteen years consists of lighting an incense cone in the morning and repeating in front of my altar:

That good luck smiles on me today and always, that my good fortune rises like the smoke of this incense, may the smoke reach every corner, and may every corner be touched by good fortune.

Candles

Candles have been associated with sorcery and witches since obscurantism, perhaps even long before. You can find them (like censers) in all colors, shapes, and sizes, and even of different materials. I recommend using wax candles because they are the most traditional. Candle magic is one of the most practical and common forms of magic that exists, and its knowledge is essential to every good sorcerer.

Candles symbolize fire and light, the effort of the human hand to mold the world to its benefit, and its natural (not electric) light is considered something almost sacred. The native shamans of the Amazon usually say *"waratshii arapuna Warattuuisü shi'ipa'aya wapüna juyaa nutuma"* (the light that man ignites in this world is visible in both worlds), alluding to the fact that every time you light a candle, it is seen in the world of the living, in the world of the spirits, and also in the veil between both worlds, thus being able to illuminate the way of the deceased souls in the beyond.

Candles alone constitute a powerful magic tool. Once you light one, its fire holds the power of desires, and according to tradition everything you write on paper and burn in the flame of a candle is a message sent to the spirit world. You can also use candles to perform all kinds of elaborate magical operations—writing on the candles about your wishes, carving magical symbols, and even using their different colors to channel different energies.

The Dagger and the Athame

These are two entirely different instruments, but they both symbolize metal as the fifth element.

A dagger is a flat blade longer than a knife and shorter than a sword that symbolizes will and courage. While some magicians and sorcerers may consider them an unnecessary weapon for the altar, their power, beyond the symbolic, is associated with protection against all kinds of evil entities. A dagger consecrated with birch oil on Saint John's Eve is a powerful tool to ward off all kinds of curses. It also has the power to exorcise evil spirits just by being present, and it is common to find it in rituals associated with removing evil entities or diverting spells back to the one who sent them.

In the 17th century book *The Treasure of the Sorcerer of St. Cyprian*, the dagger is mentioned as a ritual tool that should only be used by the most experienced master magicians. Beyond that it usually used for those spiritualistic and magical rituals associated with protecting and caring.

The *athame* has a much more ceremonial use than the dagger. But beyond its magical and ceremonial applications, it is not very common as a tool or even as a weapon. In the famous magic grimoire *The Key of Solomon*, it is mentioned as a powerful ritual tool of quite diverse uses. Additionally, in Wicca, it has gained great relevance for being employed to direct energies, a function that in the oldest ceremonial magic corresponded to the magic wand. Also in the Wiccan tradition, the athame symbolizes fire and is linked to male divinity.

Scott Cunnigham, one of the most popular authors on Wicca, suggests the use of the athame as a ceremonial instrument in several of his books. In some Internet portals we can find different recommendations about these instruments, repeatedly highlighting the use of the athame as a ceremonial instrument for men and the dagger as a ceremonial instrument for women. However, this model of thought seems somewhat dated in modern times.

In the Lucumi/Santeria esoteric tradition, in which I had the privilege of being initiated from a very young age, the use of the knife (similar to the ceremonial use of the dagger) is quite serious. It requires the performance of an entire ceremony to receive permission to employ a blade for the performance of sacrifices or certain secret rituals. While in the old magical grimoires, such as the famous book of Saint Cyprian, the use of the knife as well as other instruments requires due diligence and preparation.

So whatever instrument you want to include in your practice, take into account that this goes beyond choosing the most beautiful athame from an online store. It requires seriousness, maturity, and honoring the sacred art and veneration of the ritual sacrifices that are thousands of years old.

The Magic Wand

This tool is not only symbolic; it has a magical ritual use that, once associated with the bullying suffered by witches in the 14th century, began to be replaced by daggers, athames, and swords, as they looked for a tool that also had a greater practical utility, beyond the ritual moment.

The magic wand symbolizes trees and nature, with wood as its element, which is why wands (except for those made of quartz used in more modern holistic methods) are primarily made of materials like hazelnut, pine, cherry, hawthorn, and cedar. Wands have a variety of functions, including mixing herbal potions with magical purposes, directing and concentrating energy on a specific point or object, protecting against evil, healing, conjuring spirits, enchanting objects and other magical tools, and even predicting the weather.

Manuscripts from ancient Egypt have been found representing the God Seth with a long wand in his hand to perform spells. Another drawing, from ancient Rome, shows a wizard wielding the title of *Baculatus—The Bearer of the Wand* or *The Connoisseur of the Wand*—because *baculum* was the Roman name for a magic wand.

The wand usually receives a greater connection with the magician or sorcerer when it is made by hand, from the selection and cutting of the correct tree branch to the consecration of the same. Some magical grimoires of the 14th century suggest burying the enchanted wand for a period of seven nights before the full moon to charge it with the power of the spirits; on the other hand, it is now common to find sorcerers who prefer to decorate their wand with various crystals and wire jewelry to increase its powers. All the options are valid, but it is very important you feel the connection with the magic wand, as well as with each of the instruments you use.

The Mirror

In popular magic, mirrors are more related to clairvoyance and the creation of portals than to their more basic energy use. Mirrors reflect the light and everything around us. They are highly functional tools to achieve communication with other worlds, predict the future, and analyze dreams.

Mirrors return energy to its origin, so we place them on doors looking out when we have conflicts with a neighbor, but once at home, it is important to remember that wherever they are placed will double whatever they look upon in your life, physically and energetically speaking. That is why it is important to keep the mirrors clean of dust and impurities and to avoid having them reflect disorder, broken objects, or fire.

A mirror anointed with laurel oil will reflect all kinds of hexes hidden in the light. A walnut-framed mirror reflects ill-intentioned spirits on its surface. A hand mirror with a five-pointed star engraved on the wooden handle will bend the will of any spirit, and a hand mirror with a *Rub el Hizb* symbol, or the eight-pointed *Star of Solomon* protects from all kinds of spirits in your ritual space.

If you prefer to keep your ritual space free of reflections, you can simply anoint a piece of dark cloth with camphor oil and use it to cover any mirror in your magical space. According to the very common spiritual teaching in South America where the mirrors are washed with camphor water, this also prevents spirits and other entities that have not been invoked from entering this earthly plane through the mirror.

Your Personal Tool as a Mage

Every good mage has a power tool they keep with them. This tool can be a ring, a bracelet, a necklace, an old key, even a staff—something that in this physical plane is virtually anchored to the mage—hence its power is an extension of the mage's.

This tool or instrument is an anchor to the mage's power, a totem with his own energy, which they may well use as an extra battery to charge spells, to protect from the energies of someone else who has bad intentions, or to assign it a specific power, for example, the attraction of good fortune and abundance.

This is not a task that is carried out lightly. To consecrate your own magic tool, it is necessary that you have an object with which you have a strong affinity. This can be achieved in two ways. First, this object (a ring, necklace, or other item) has been with you for years and is more than a decorative element for you, because it is loaded with important symbolic and emotional value. Or second, this instrument is manufactured by your own hands, like a ceramic or iron coin, some jewelry with crystals you bought on a trip, an amulet that you made many years ago and is still with you, and so on.

Once you have the instrument in your hands, you will need to perform the consecration ritual, but if you are going to carry out the consecration or enchantment of this magical object for your personal use, I suggest two things:

» Choose an important or significant date for you, such as your birthday, an anniversary, or even an eclipse (astrological events are loaded with enormous power.

» Draw or carve your name and some magical symbol on the object, such as a pentagram, sun, moon, your zodiac sign, or other personally significant symbol.

Your tools are under your command at all times, which is why it is best for you to consecrate them. You should be involved in the whole process, at least as much as possible. And although many of these tools can be obtained in a store or via the Internet, do not forget that the more intimate your relationship with the creation of the tool, the greater your connection to its energy, and the better the long-term effects.

Consecrating Your Tools

I have given you a complete list of tools to keep in mind, obviously you do not need them all, only those that you consider necessary to carry out your purposes. But whatever you choose to keep with you, they must be consecrated. Here is the proper way to do it.

CONSECRATION RITUAL

You will need:
- » A clean and tidy space
- » Green, red, and yellow chalk
- » Eight white candles
- » A big bowl
- » Coarse salt
- » Rose incense
- » Eight white or translucent quartz crystals
- » Essential oils of sandalwood, myrrh, and cedar

Step 1

In the space you have chosen, draw a wide circle with green, red, and yellow chalk wide enough to sit inside it, and a second smaller circle within it. Inside the central circle, draw two squares on top of each other, forming an eight-pointed star. At each point of the star place a white candle.

Step 2

Fill the bowl with the coarse salt, light the incense, place your hands in the bowl, and massage the salt with your hands, pronouncing out loud "this space is sacred, this space is blessed, this space is protected." Throw the salt around you, inside and outside the circle, to activate its energy. Throw the salt from the height of your shoulders, not above you.

Step 3

Light the white candles. Enter the circle taking each of the crystals with you. Anoint the crystals with the oils and take them one by one with your hands. Place the crystal on your heart with both hands and repeat in a low voice "you are charged, you are blessed and protected," and repeat this brief spell with each of the eight crystals. As you do, place each crystal within the central circle with the star.

Step 4

Once the candles and incense are burning, the crystals are properly charged and connected with you, take each of the tools and place them inside the central circle very carefully, and recite with each of the tools

I consecrate you and conjure you, I bless you and I protect you, may it be my energy that makes you beat and may my ancestors be the ones who make you live, I activate you and I consecrate you as a powerful tool to manifest my power, that as long as you are with me nothing is missing and nothing bad happens, you are a powerful amulet, you are a powerful tool, and your growing power is a reflection of my constantly growing power.

Final Step

At the end of pronouncing the spell properly with each of the tools you have, collect them and sweep the circle. Keep the tools that you have consecrated in a space near the altar and keep the quartz crystals that you have consecrated wrapped in cloth. You can use these same crystals in the future to consecrate other magical tools, either for you or for someone else.

As of this moment your tools are duly consecrated.

Extra Tips

Some people prefer to carry out these rituals with the new moon, thus symbolizing the beginning of something new, and perform a second consecration (rather a kind of confirmation) of the tools, when they complete the first three months. It's not mandatory, but it is a good tip for the most dedicated.

In my personal practice, I add a few drops of blood from a finger of my left hand to the oil blend every time I perform the consecration of an amulet, talisman, or magic tool. It is not mandatory and depends on the belief and magical foundations of each individual. If you are willing to do it, it is important to be very careful, use a sterilized needle, and properly clean the skin before the ritual.

I use large quartz crystals to carry out this ritual, but if you wish, you can use stones chosen by you personally from a river or beach. The important thing is the symbolism of earth in the ritual, and the quartz crystals add an extra energy to each spell you perform.

Your Personal Book of Magic

For some mages the most important tool of all may be the cauldron where they prepare their potions, concoctions, and mixtures of oils. For many others it is the wand as an extension of their power. For others it is the dagger or the athame as a representation of the power that is imposed to change the course of things, while many say that their most powerful tool is their faith in their work. From my point of view faith is what will drive you, it is your engine, but it is not a tool. You do not use faith.

One very powerful tool that will grow in conjunction with you day after day is your magic diary. Along with your dream journal where you write down those nighttime visions of the astral journey that you make voluntarily or involuntarily every night, your magic diary, your individual recipe book, is where you will write down and draw your rituals and spells. It is where you record every detail of the rituals you plan to do on Samhain or the Winter Solstice. It is where you will write that recipe for love that has worked very well for you, that protection spell you placed on your loved ones, or that magical ritual to perform with your group on the new or full moon. It is there, in that notebook, you will write your premonitions, your auguries, your rituals of celebration, your personal growth spells, and the astrological events that you consider relevant.

Your spell and enchantment diary (or whatever you wish to call it) is perhaps your primary tool, because it is those pages that will reflect (not for others, but for yourself) the result of your individual growth as a mage and sorcerer, as a practitioner and as conjurer of the elements of nature, abundance, and the old gods of good fortune.

But don't get me wrong, your spell book must be a reflection of yourself and your learning, although the old conception of the huge, antique-looking book with ribbons to separate the thick pages and the perfect illustrations in every corner can be very romantic. Today, perhaps, we live much busier lives.

I started out with several magic notebooks written in pencil, coloring each page by hand one by one. But I have reached the point of storing many of my enchantments on CDs, flash drives, memory cards, even in a small private blog in the cloud that only I can access—or at least I think so!

You can open a Word file on your laptop and from there, start taking notes. Write down your lunar calendar, your birth chart, your rituals and spells, your recipes for the Sabbath, and anything else that's important for your journey.

You can have more than just one book of magic. I have many, including a notebook covered in blue cloth, filled with spells and rituals that I have copied there from other books and grimoires that have crossed my path. While my personal spellbook is full of enchantments, rituals, invocations, and names of spirits that were hard to obtain, many came in exchange for various favors.

Open your arms before you sleep at night

to release and dismiss all excess and hinders.

Open your arms when you wake up in the morning

to embrace all that you've been asking for.

Open your arms in the morning,

to everything that you have forgotten to ask for.

3

THE SUN, MOON, AND PLANETS IN MAGIC

The influence of the lunar and solar phases in each of your magical works

---

From the origins of humanity, our race has admired the movements of the Sun and the Moon with great curiosity and interest. The first magicians and astrologers in Egypt learned to predict the future by looking at the clouds and subsequently understood that those omens in the clouds of Heaven were just a vague and ephemeral translation of the predictions that were much further away in the stars. Since then astrology has always been linked to sorcery and magic, because whether the mage knows it or not, the effects of the stars and planets on his spells will be there regardless. That is why considering the different movements of the stars and planets through the sky for your various spells will help you achieve a greater effect.

The Sun, in magic and sorcery, is linked to the external self, the events that occur in the day-to-day of the physical world, and our physiological reaction to each of these events.

The Moon, on the other hand, is linked to the subconscious, our inner selves, deep understanding and divine wisdom, and the events that occur in the inner plane and the way we understand them.

The phases of the sun change according to the seasons and the hours and rule over the day and the elements of fire, earth, and light. The phases of the moon change month by month and cover darkness, waters, wind, and our understanding of time.

In simpler words, if your spells are linked to solar energy, land, energy, and physical health, as well as magical works related to the spirits, gods, and avatars of fire and earth, or to affect the consciousness of someone else, these jobs tend to gain more strength if you consider the Sun.

For spells and rituals that work with lunar energy magic linked to water and undines, wind and air nymphs such as faeries and silfides, magical works performed at night and in darkness, and those works that have effects on the subconscious (premonitory dreams, mental health, trauma healing), the most appropriate thing is to consider the phases of the moon.

The Sun is visible at all times and nearly every day of the year. We use the sun to count our days, and its movement is associated with the four seasons. During winter the Sun is farther from the Earth and its energy is distant. Magical works done in this season take longer to complete and their effects are slow and smooth, but once spring begins, the magical works associated with the Sun gain strength and feed on its energy, while those rituals performed during the summer and autumn (especially in summer) are nourished by the energy of the Star King that is closer and more constant.

Now, with respect to the hours of the day, the most appropriate times for works associated with the energy of the sun are between the morning, about two hours after dawn, and the afternoon, about two hours before sunset, so they will be charged with force and effect more immediate than others performed at night.

However, in sorcery it is more common to work with the Moon and its phases than with the Sun. I recommend being clear about the energy you are working with, and identifying whether it is solar or lunar energy is important.

In terms of abundance, if the Sun is the creator of fortune and success, it is important that you work with its energy and symbolism to attract money and abundance. If the Moon is the one who manages and distributes the energy of good fortune, it is important to use those lunar phases to carry out rituals and empower amulets that seek to keep money (savings and investments) and to keep it fluidly walking between us.

Solar Energy

The Sun is constantly creating light day after day. It is a living organism that has its own consciousness, mind, purpose, and even its own loves.

The Sun in charge of divine creation, and it brings us its creative light and powerful energy to motivate us and push us to manifest our new reality, our own abundance, and our purpose.

All of us carry the Sun and Moon within us, and our power of manifestation is a reflection of that. Once we understand this old truth, we will able to connect with our stars, their powerful energy, and our manifestation's purpose.

The golden energy is linked to the Golden Lord (the Sun), the king of our stars and our mornings, who, from dawn to dusk, can be seen with his bright crown in the sky.

The Sun is also connected with all those tasks that in human history were more strongly associated with masculinity, such as hunting, physical strength, and dexterity. It is a dominant but also impulsive energy. Along with the sun, volcanoes and earthquakes are strongly linked to this golden-colored energy.

The Moon on the other hand, looks calm and silent, almost lifeless; however it is the moon who brings balance to life, who illuminates the nights when the sun is not visible, who takes, calms, and filters the energy. Both are just as necessary to celebrate the cycles of nature and give life to everything that walks and breathes on earth. Therefore, it is important to understand that both are part of a delicate balance, and working with both will bring you the balance you may need.

So it is the Golden Lord, the creator of all the energy and warm, golden light, that nourishes the earth, plants, and all living beings and prevents our world from becoming another huge frozen planet, but it is the Silver Queen who during other hours takes the energy of the sun that does not reach us, cleanses and purifies it, nourishes it with its own vibration, and from that pale surface sends it to light our nights and nurture the earth.

Lunar Energy

Lunar energy is linked to the lady of the dark sky, the queen and mother of all the creatures that walk in the night, and also of the plants that grow and bloom in the absence of the sun.

If today the sun is the dominant father due to the work we perform during daylight hours, it is worth remembering that ancient humanity took refuge in the dark caves seeking the protection of that nocturnal mother who watched over our ancestors who feared the wild beasts of the day.

Lunar energy is connected to magic performed at night, and due to its association with the feminine, it is the moon who governs what used to be considered women's work, including home and family care, cooking, and the arts as well as reasoning and good use of logic.

In times when society broke the natural balance due to political-religious issues that considered women inferior, the moon wandered the world leaving its mark on each religion where women were associated with mysticism and sorcery, because the Moon gave them the tools and knowledge they needed to care for their families and loved ones.

The energy of the moon is associated with darkness, shadows, night, and the hidden mysteries within them. When you perform any kind of spell destined to have any effect on the unconscious, premonitory dreams, spiritual vision, the ability to deploy your astral body outside your physical body, or your relationship with the spirit world, the phases of the moon will have an almost intimate effect on these rituals, because you are working within their domains. The more you understand the Moon and its powers, the better results you will get.

Lunar Phases

I invite you to learn from the moon, which illuminates but does not disturb, influences all but does not force things, and stands firm and proud in her corner of the sky.

NEW MOON

Symbolizes nothingness, inner reflection, and spiritual awakening.

This is the time to reflect and meditate, plan the realization of spells, organize social meetings with other sorcerers, and sow growth intentions in the short term. It is a time to devote yourself to studying other forms of magic and meditation. It is when the magic that allows you to introduce yourself through dreams to other worlds becomes stronger.

WAXING MOON

Symbolizes the beginning of something new, learning, and the unconscious.

The waxing moon symbolizes the growth of something and the evolution of a process. It is when you perform those rituals and enchantments that deal with manifesting something new in the short term, increasing someone else's feelings, growing a project, or going deeper into a process of personal change. If you want to perform a ritual to increase the faith of your partners in a joint project, your clairvoyance, your ability to learn, or perform any kind of transformation in yourself or someone else, this is the right moon.

FULL MOON

Symbolizes physical and spiritual maturity, personal achievement, and wisdom.

Here we find the moon at its greatest and most imposing moment, its force is so powerful that it feels like a gigantic sea wave that throws you against the rocks. It has the power to create all kinds of changes in the short and long term (including with leaders and governments), generate internal and external transformations of all kinds, and facilitate work with spirits, rituals of personal growth, the culmination of long-term spells, even those spells to transform another individual's form or thought. All those rituals gain strength on the full moon.

WANING MOON

Symbolizes introspection, the closing of a cycle, the final transformation, and death.

The waning phase occurs when the moon has stopped growing and maturing, it is here that its light begins to enter the world of spirits. Nights become darker, its influence decreases, and its power seems to lessen progressively. Use this moon for the realization of spells and rituals that seek to end something, destroy something, cancel a spell, give up bad habits, remove someone, or abandon something important in your life that you thought necessary but has already fulfilled its function.

The Moon in Each Sign

The sun has influence over all that is so visible as daylight—but moon, oh moon, you are the one who influences what we ignore, forget, and hide.

THE MOON IN THE FIRE SIGNS

These are the lunar positions that involve the competitive spirit, team triumph, the success of a project, and business growth.

Moon in Aries
Use to perform magical works linked to personal value, freedom, overcoming challenges and obstacles, enthusiasm, and authority.

Moon in Leo
Use to carry out all those magical works linked to the world of art and entertainment, fame, cultural affairs, trust, creativity, prestige, and material wealth.

Moon in Sagittarius
Use for all those rituals and amulets destined to protect the traveler and the merchant, the immigrant and the connoisseur of new lands and other languages, to open roads, and the search for a personal path.

THE MOON IN THE EARTH SIGNS

The moon in the earth signs promotes firmness, stability, eloquence, and character.

Moon in Taurus
This moon will add strength to all those spells linked to achieving firmness in the field of love and money, couple stability, the search for a new job, personal fulfillment, and sensuality.

Moon in Virgo
This moon is best for works that involve order and organization, from a ritual to rearrange your altar to a spell to balance the energy of the home. Also those spells linked to health, internal and external healing processes, and emotional healing gain special strength in this lunar cycle.

Moon in Capricorn
This is a protective moon par excellence. Use it to perform rituals and spells to protect yourself, your loved ones, family, pets and friends, rituals to protect the home, the workplace, the vehicle, and even economic investments.

THE MOON IN THE AIR SIGNS

The moon in air signs powers communication. Communication between couples, friends, family members, and even with bosses, executives, managers, judges, lawyers, and publishers is positive.

Moon in Gemini

This moon favors those spells and rituals for harmony in the home or workplace, the exchange of information, the unification of a group, truth, dissemination of information and knowledge, and communication. All get a boost of strength, especially those rituals that you can create to publicize something new, such as a book, a project, or a new place.

Moon in Libra

Use this moon to balance and correct the order of things. Spells linked to justice, diplomacy, politics, and the search for balance gain strength under this moon.

Moon in Aquarius

This is the most human and idealistic phase of the moon. For these times, I recommend you perform rituals to make your own personality, creativity, and social and humanitarian aid shine. It also does well for idealism and the search for your own place in the world.

THE MOON IN THE WATER SIGNS

This is the moon that favors all those magical works carried out in close proximity to rivers, lakes, and beaches, and also all those rituals linked to the world of dreams, the spiritual plane, and psychic energy.

Moon in Cancer

This moon phase favors clairvoyance, divination, and precognition, all of those rituals that seek to investigate the hidden, reveal secrets, find lost things and people, and immerse yourself in the world of shadows and dreams.

Moon in Scorpio

This is the phase of the moon that is linked to the past, trips to the past through the world of dreams, spiritual sessions, Ouija sessions, and retrocognitions. It is also the moon that allows us to perform spells to immerse ourselves in our own being, know ourselves better, and heal from within.

Moon in Pisces

This is one of the most spiritual moons, along with Virgo, and one of the moons with the greatest link to the esoteric world, along with Scorpio. All those spells that are performed to change something in someone's mind, a thought, a feeling, a way of thinking, a prejudice or a memory, gain special strength when performed under the moon in Pisces.

The sun and the moon do not complain about the light of the stars, in the same way the stars do not envy the light of the moon and the sun, on the contrary, they take it, make it their own, reflect it, and distribute it in other directions. What you give to the universe finds beautiful ways to return to you, just as the light reflects back to the stars.

Planetary Energies

Just as our months are governed by various sun signs, the days of the week are governed by the various planets. These daily correspondences, despite being drawn largely from the tradition of the old alchemists, have inevitably been integrated into the magic language of modern sorcery. Although there is no problem with performing any ritual when it is most comfortable for you, doing the rituals taking into account the moon phases as well as the days' correspondences, will provide better results in various ways. For example:

Suppose an individual we will call Santiago (one of my favorite names) has a liver problem and is undergoing strict medical treatment to promote healing, but Santiago has recently taken up witchcraft in its most traditional form. He only uses traditional white candles and does not follow the phases of the moon or the correspondences of days.

Santiago decides to perform a healing ritual using white candles on a Tuesday (a day ruled astrologically by Mars) to help his liver treatment progress. This should not have been a problem, except that Mars, the ruling planet of that day, is more focused on taking action, promoting the execution of accurate plans and strategies for war or marketing. This planet of war also promotes arguing and bleeding. Santiago might strengthen his medical treatment with this ritual, but his progress may be slower than expected—functional, yes, but slow.

The following Tuesday, Santiago is admitted to the emergency room because the treatment has not been working as expected. We could say that his ritual worked because he had to abandon a treatment that was destined to last months, or years, for a surgery that quickly cured his discomfort but cost him all his savings and left him unable to work for several weeks.

But now, let's suppose that Irene (another fictional character with another name that I really like) has the same problem as Santiago, and she, with perhaps a little more experience, decides to perform a healing ritual, taking into account everything she has learned during years of study. She acquires the necessary elements for her ritual days before. She knows the best time to start something is the new moon, but because it is two weeks away, she performs the ritual starting on Wednesday and continuing into Thursday, days that are ruled by Mercury (the planet of communications and doctors) and Jupiter (the planet of greatness and personal success).

Irene uses a combination of white and green candles in her ritual to heal herself from within and promote a rapid recovery with the energy of the earth. On Thursday she focuses on performing *several short meditations, lights some blue and green candles for her speedy recovery, and ends each sentence with, "May everything that happens be for my own good. Thank you!"*

Most likely, Irene has a quicker, less serious recovery without prolonged ailments or surprises because Mercury and Jupiter align everything in her favor to promote good communication with her doctors, ensure the medications she orders online do not get lost in the mail, and her body responds properly to the treatment, plus her insurance may even decide to cover all expenses so Irene can continue saving without having to pay for a very expensive recovery.

This does not mean that all the rituals you perform without taking into account these elements are wrong—on the contrary, they are very well done, because they are done from the heart—but by complementing them in this way, you can greatly improve your results.

Sunday

Sunday is ruled by the Sun, the Star King generator of light and vital energy, and as such, this day is also ruled by all the gods and deities associated with the sun and sacred fire. Rituals and spells associated with solar energy gain greater force on this day, including forms of magic that work with light, daytime, fire, vital energy, empowerment, masculine energy, virility, healing of animals, plants, and pets. The sun also has dominion over those rituals linked to well-known gods that are worshiped in broad daylight, such as Apollo, Helios, Athena, Oshun, and other deities from different pantheons.

Monday

Monday is governed by the lunar deities, and they administer and direct the energy of this day. For that reason on Monday we perform those rituals and spells that are associated with sensitivity, intuition, divination arts, prophetic dreams, and all those magical works associated with the psychic world and the kingdoms of dreams or spirits.

This is the best day to try your first spell and gain recognition from the spirit world. This day is also intimately linked with the female universe, making it a good day to raise your prayers related to women's rights, femininity, fertility, motherhood, and mother-daughter or mother-son ties.

According to the spiritualist tradition, it is advisable to light white candles on Monday nights, in order to illuminate the path of the spirits and the deceased toward the beyond, allowing them to move on and not get stuck in the world of the living.

Tuesday

Tuesday is the day ruled by the planet Mars and the old gods of war. The Romans considered Mars a god of war and brute force because he promoted a state of excitement and euphoria in soldiers during battle. Today he is known as a god of action and impulse, which is why Tuesday is the day we perform rituals and spells to help us act on an issue, solve a problem, or regain control of something we have lost—a company, a house, a family situation, an academic project, and the like.

This day also energetically governs everything that is linked to blood and sexuality; therefore, rituals intended for both areas must be performed with accurate care, because Mars is a deity who likes to end problems from the root. And once he senses you working on something in his domain during his watch, it will not take long for him to intervene to find a way to eradicate the problem have, even without your consent or prayers.

The best rituals you can perform this day are those that promote physical energy, will, sexual vigor, and health. It is also a day to solve a personal issue, avoid an upcomming conflict, or keep someone away.

Wednesday

Wednesday is the day ruled energetically by Mercury, the messenger of the gods. He rules communications, the intellect, travelers and their ways, paperwork and passports, immigrants and merchants; he is also considered the god of thieves for being the only god who heeded their pleas when they prayed not to be persecuted, imprisoned, or punished for their actions. Mercury also governs society in general and the ways of information, commerce, and communication. Therefore, all things having to do with those disciplines are elements under the tutelage of this day.

Rituals linked to promoting your understanding of an issue and helping you become more spontaneous and sociable, better understand social and commercial relationships, increase the flow of money, mobilize bank accounts, take care of your savings, and get investors gain more force when they are performed on a Wednesday. Lighting blue and green candles in a shop or office in the early hours of a Wednesday is a good way to attract customers and move money in a positive direction.

Thursday

Thursday is the day ruled by Jupiter, the king of all gods, kings, and men—a judge who rules over everything with an iron fist and who is not afraid to punish or reward gods and men alike according to their actions. He was also envied and even betrayed by several of his children, but never surpassed or replaced. If you identify with Jupiter in any of these aspects, if you feel that you are about to be replaced, fired, betrayed, or deceived, and you are in charge of a company, a home, a foundation, or a family, this is the day to invoke his strength and constancy.

Thursday is the most appropriate day to promote justice, laws, and personal or family greatness. Any rituals you perform hoping to get recognition from others, solve legal issues, or promote successful meetings with a lawyer gain extra force when performed on this day.

If you are about to get a promotion, a new position in your workplace, or start a new academic career, light blue candles with your name written on them to win the favor of Jupiter and his perseverance.

Friday

Friday is the day ruled by Venus. In roman mythology Venus is the goddess of beauty and love—passionate, personal, and individual. In astrology Venus is associated with charisma, self-esteem, desire, and the search for love and affection.

All rituals associated with love, affection, and self-esteem gain greater strength when performed on this day. The energy of Venus favors those magical works that attract love and strengthen the bonds between members of a couple, as well as spells to care for our loved ones or increase the strength of our desire to attract something with greater force.

Saturday

This is the day ruled by Saturn, the king of karma, structure, and order, the eternal ruler of times past. Saturn also governs personal and professional projects. On this day, rituals linked to establishing and strengthening structures and hierarchies, long-term projects and other endeavors, academic studies that are about to start, and intentions of growth become stronger.

Saturday is the most appropriate day to perform rituals that focus on supporting or strengthening a new project, a new process, or a new course that you are about to embark upon.

4

GODS AND SPIRITS OF ABUNDANCE, WEALTH, AND YOUR RELATIONSHIP WITH THEM

And it paid the cost
And it cries every step of the way
And nobody believed in what it was doing
And it left its home, its family, its comfort zone
And set out on this road alone
And it started with fear
And the cost was much, the cost was a lot, the cost was everything
And it broke every one of its bones in the process
And it thought it had died.

And finally one day it woke up
And spread its wings
And embarked on a journey that its past could not understand

And already then its loved ones did not want it anymore
And then it had changed, it was distant, it was strange.
But it was no longer its responsibility to justify oneself
It had grown, it had changed, it had evolved
Now it had wings, and now the children drew it
And now it adorned the wind with the color of its wings.
                    —On the Butterfly's Head, Elhoim Leafar

Myths and folklore have given us a long list of gods and spirits well known in various cultures of the world. These gods, avatars, spirits, and entities encompass all kinds of archetypes and natural events. From the moment something new arises, something is created, something is transformed, an avatar arises to take control of that event and become its corresponding god.

We have gods of communication, commerce, medicine, poetry, wisdom, stars, oceans, earthquakes, love, war, and misfortune. All these immortal entities that embody a principle, a law, an archetype, or an event, are present wherever they are summoned, including the gods of abundance, wealth, good fortune, and well-being, which are listed below.

All these gods and goddesses are wonderful in their own way, and depending on your region, you can make a small altar for the god of your choice or for any other gods or goddesses on the list.

The Gods and Spirits

For millennia humanity has found in gods and spirits the answer to their pleas, their many questions, and that light at the end of the tunnel. Although the gods are many in number, many of their names remain unknown.

Gods and Goddesses of Good Fortune

ABUNDANTIA

Abundantia is the Roman goddess of success, wealth, and prosperity. During the Golden Age she was one of the so-called *Virtues*, manifested as the figure of a robust and very cheerful woman, always sitting, smiling, and carrying with her the sacred cornucopia (the symbol of abundance). Her cult is still present to this day in much of Europe.

According to certain experts, scholars, and anthropologists, other goddesses such as Rosmerta and Domina were incarnations of Abundantia in different periods and for different peoples.

ASTARTE

Astarte is a Phoenician-Canaanite goddess of life, fertility, love, and carnal pleasures. Her cult represented the cult of Mother Nature, as she was considered an embodiment of her. Astarte was also venerated as a goddess of war, but her ceremonial role as goddess of fertility and the cycles of the earth survives to this day.

BONUS EVENTUS AND LYMPHA

This couple was, for the Romans, the archetype of a prosperous family in a good city. Bonus Eventus was originally revered as the god of agriculture, a benevolent deity who distributed goods and brought good omens in exchange for the horses that were sacrificed to him in October.

Lympha was the goddess of fresh water and one of the most relevant water goddesses of her time. Later both became part of the twelve agricultural deities well revered by farmers, and as a couple they embodied prosperity and good trade.

CERES

Ceres is the Roman goddess of agriculture, crops, fertility, and cereals (which received their name from her). Ceres taught humanity the art of cultivating the land, sowing, collecting wheat, and making bread.

The cult of Ceres was so important to the Romans that twelve other minor gods of agriculture were considered by the Roman tradition as the advisors and helpers of the goddess in her work. Pigs, wild boars, and rams were sacrificed in her name during the holidays.

DEDUN

Dedun was initially revered as the god of incense in the old Middle Kingdom of Egypt (around 2400 BC). He was also linked to funeral rites and was the protector of the deceased rulers of Nubia.

The burning of incense, a mystical tradition from Nubia, became a very important ceremony in the king's rooms to purify the air and scare away evil spirits. Due to the extremely expensive materials and manufacture of incense at that time, its trade brought great prosperity to Nubia. From there Nubians and others in that region began to revere Dedun as the god of prosperity, trade, abundance, and good fortune.

DEMETER (THE MOTHER GODDESS)

Demeter was the goddess of the poppies and sister of the king of the gods, Zeus, to the first Greeks. She and her daughter Persephone were the two goddesses of nature and food, well known at that time as *the Demeter* or *to theo* (the two goddesses). When her daughter was kidnapped by Hades and dragged into the underworld to become his queen, Demeter hid the sun and sent the icy winds over the world's crops, creating the autumn and subsequent winter.

While looking for her daughter in the form of an old woman, she taught Triptólemo (son of King Celeo) the art of agriculture, and, through him, the rest of Greece learned to plant, tend the land, and harvest crops, whereby Demeter became revered as the goddess of agriculture and everything green. From a subsequent agreement with Hades to spend six months a year with her daughter, Demeter created the seasonal cycles and also called the seasons.

Having mixed among men to teach them to sow the seeds and cultivate the land, she earned a larger title that remains to this day—the Greek goddess of agriculture, the bearer of the seasons, and the Lady of All Grains, and Nourisher of the Land. Demeter also symbolizes the transforming cycle of life and death.

DOMINA ABUNDIA

Domina Abundia is a local goddess of abundance and wealth with a little known cult among the old cities of France and Italy between 1300 and 1500. In homes where she is revered food and money are never lacking.

Domina Abundia is associated with the cult of the dominae, a set of nymphs, spirits, or semi gods that were venerated by the local priests inside their homes but not in the temples. According to their folklore, they visited the houses where they were venerated at night after making sure that all the inhabitants slept, then proceeded to eat all the food on the table, but the plates and glasses of those who ate and drank were never emptied. In this way they would never lack wealth or food in the home.

LAKSHMI (लकषमी)

Lakshmi is the mother goddess, goddess of beauty, providence, and good luck in Hinduism. For Buddhists, she is the goddess of abundance, protection, and good fortune. She represents the material world and is the eternal consort of the god Vishnu.

FORTUNA

Fortuna is the Roman goddess of good luck and fertility, and also of bad luck and misfortune. In myth she was considered the most capricious goddess on Olympus, who presided over all events and also distributed, according to her whim, the goods and evils to humanity.

Poets and artists used to represent her bald and blind, standing and with two wings on both feet, one on a spinning wheel (the wheel of fortune) and the other in the air (freedom). Sometimes she has a sun and crescent on her head indicating that just like the stars, fortune presides over everything that happens on earth.

KUBERA (कुबेर)

Kubera is the Hindu god of wealth—the lord, connoisseur, and owner of all the world's treasures, the god-king of the semidivine *laksás* (benevolent spirits), and the treasurer of the gods. He is considered the *dikpala* that protects the north (one of the four protectors of the directions) and a *lokapalá* (protector of the world).

NURTIA

Nurtia is the Etruscan goddess of fate, luck, opportunity, and good fortune.

OSHUN (ÒṢUN)

Oshun is the Yoruba goddess (an Orixa) of love, good fortune, abundance, money, luxury, and fresh water. She is the queen of the world, streams, springs, and rivers. She manifests herself as a beautiful African woman in a dress—sometimes yellow, sometimes white—many times wearing flowers in her hair and carrying a jar filled with fresh river water.

It is Oshun who attends to monetary matters, resolves debts, and helps people get jobs or clients. It is common to find her image in commercial premises and all kinds of businesses where her presence is evoked to attract good fortune.

PLUTO (THE DIVINE CHILD)

Pluto is the Greek god of riches and hidden treasures, agriculture, and abundance. Zeus left him blind to pay and favor mortals without any prejudice.

ROSMERTA (THE GREAT PROVIDER)

Rosmerta is the Celtic goddess of fertility and abundance. There are numerous statues of Rosmerta throughout France and over twenty-seven inscriptions and stone engravings with her image and name found in France, Germany, and Luxembourg. In these representations we find the goddess carrying a bag full of food or a basket of fruit, often with a ceremonial plate or a cornucopia in one hand, and often accompanied by Mercury, the god of commerce and travelers.

Rosmerta's cult included filling a basket with fruit and flowers in honor of the goddess and placing it by the door to welcome her arrival, In this way she would fill the site with her blessings, and they would never lack anything.

TYQUE

Tyque is the Greek goddess of fate, fortune, luck, and prosperity. She was portrayed as a beautiful blind woman sitting on the wheel of fortune always unsure of her decisions. Her father Oceano gave Tyque the divine right to decide the fate of any mortal, and she did it in a random way, with the help of Pluto, the god of wealth. When a man boasted of his own luck and wealth without thanking the gods, Tyque sent Nemesis, goddess of justice and divine punishment, to punish him.

UNNEFERTH (PERFECT BEFORE AND AFTER AFTER BIRTH)

Unneferth or Usur, is the Egyptian god of resurrection, vegetation, agriculture, and a symbol of the fertility and regeneration of the Nile. His father was Geb and his mother was Nut. The ancient Egyptians attributed the invention of wine to him.

After dying, Unneferth was resurrected and later revered also as the god of the dead and resurrection, playing an extremely important role in the court of judgment of the deceased in Egyptian mythology. He was also considered the god of the renewal and regeneration of crops and wine. He is known in the West by his Hellenic name, Osiris.

ZHAO GONG (赵公明 / GOD OF WEALTH)

Zhao Gong is a venerable god of fortune and wealth in traditional Chinese religion, Taoism, and Tibetan Buddhism. He rules over good fortune, gambling, health, well-being, and alchemy. For this last reason he is represented carrying an instrument capable of turning iron into gold.

The Seven Gods of Fortune

These are the seven gods of health, well-being, and good fortune in Japanese folklore. Several of them are well known in the West thanks to popular worship, feng shui books, and for being easily found in restaurants, shops, and local Asian trade.

The seven gods of fortune have a cult that has not stopped growing for more than a thousand years, managing to break down cultural and linguistic borders, becoming venerated today by merchants from all over the world.

The author Chiba Reiko in his book *The Seven Lucky Gods of Japan* compiles the *Takarabune* legend, according to which, during the first three days of each year, the seven divinities embark from the skies on a ship named *Takarabune* carrying treasures and bringing them to human ports.

The founding gods of this divine ensemble were Ebisu and Daikokuten, both of whom were gods of business and commerce well-worshiped by the local merchants of Japan. Several of these gods are more modern manifestations, incarnations, or variations of other gods in Asia.

EBISU (恵比寿)

Ebisu, the only god of purely Japanese origin, is the god of prosperity, abundance, and wealth in business, crops, and grain. He is the patron saint of fishermen and workers; therefore he is represented wearing fishermen's clothing including a typical fisherman's hat, a fishing rod in his right hand, and holding a fish, usually a carp, hake, cod, or sea bass.

DAIKOKUTEN (大黒天)

Daikokuten is the god of commerce and prosperity, other characteristics attributed to him being patron saint of cooks, bankers, and farmers, protector of the crops of the earth, and a demon hunter. This god is always shown smiling, having short legs, and wearing a hat on his head. He usually carries a sack full of valuables or a magic mallet of good luck.

BISHAMONTEN (毘沙門天)

Bishamonten is a manifestation of the Hindu God-King Kúbera, also known as Vaisravana. He is one of the Four Heavenly Kings of the Buddhist universe, the god of good fortune in war and battles, and also related to authority and dignity. He is the protector god of those who follow the rules and behave correctly, and also of sacred and other important places. He carries a pagoda in his left hand and a spear to fight against evil spirits in his right hand.

BENZAITEN (弁財天)

Benzaiten, a Japanese Buddhist goddess is the only woman among the first gods of Japanese folklore. She is the patron goddess of music and fine arts, knowledge, and beauty. She is native to India and a manifestation of the Hindu Goddess Sarasvati. She is represented as an intelligent and beautiful woman carrying a *biwa*, a traditional Japanese lute-like instrument. She is also usually accompanied by a white snake.

FUKUROKUJU (福禄寿)

Fukurokuju, the god of wisdom, luck, longevity, wealth, and happiness, was one of the Chinese philosophers who could live without eating and the only god who has been credited with the ability to raise the dead. He is originally from China and considered a reincarnation of the Taoist God Hsuan-wu. Fukurokuju is characterized by the size of his face, being almost as large as his body, and by representing himself in traditional Chinese clothing, carrying a cane in one hand and a parchment in the other, with writings on the knowledge of the world. This god is usually accompanied by a turtle, a crow, or a deer.

JUROJIN (寿老人)

Jurojin is the embodiment of the southern polar star *Nankyokusei* and the god of old age and longevity in the mythology of Japanese Buddhism. He is known by his rather long head and long white beard, being mounted on a deer, and often accompanied by a 1,500-year-old crane and a turtle, thus expressing his affinity for long life. In his hands he holds a staff with a scroll tied to it.

HOTEI (布袋)

Hotei is the god of fortune, the guardian and protector of children, and patron of fortune-tellers and innkeepers. He is also the god of popularity and abundance. He is depicted as a smiling, bald, fat man with a curly mustache. His belly sticks out between his clothes, so he always seems to be half naked.

Before being deified during the Edo period, Hotei was a Zen priest by the name of Kaishi who died in AD 916.

KICHIJŌTEN OR KISSHOUTENNYO (吉祥天 / THE EIGHTH DEITY)

Kichijōten Japanese goddess of beauty, happiness, and fertility is also the Buddhist incarnation of the Hindu Goddess Lakshmi. In different currents of more modern worship her sacred figure replaces other gods such as Jurojin or Fukurokuju, thus assuming a place among the seven gods of fortune.

Spirits of Wealth and Wishes

THE PROSPEROUS

The Prosperous are a group of semidivine spirits without specific names that intervene in your life according to your wishes. These spirits of light, similar to the Arab djinn and the faeries of medieval tales, act like small, forceful workers greater than karma, and they have the responsibility to act on thinking beings according to the quality of their actions.

These spirits of light are well known in the holistic world of spiritualism, and they are the ones that assist you once you make a wish to "no one in particular," such as a wish made while blowing out a birthday candle, on the first star in the sky, or on a coin picked up from the street.

It is they who listen to the desire and put into action the whole process to ensure the desire is fulfilled. That is if, based on your real actions, they will move in favor of granting the desire instead of against it. According to oral tradition, they are not very good at understanding or feeling any empathy, they simply work to grant the wishes that have been requested and transmit them to a force greater than themselves—the god corresponding to the necessary attribute.

For example, if a child makes the secret wish by blowing out a birthday candle that he wants to see a faery, one of these spirits will receive that wish and do his best to carry it out. The spirit only understands that the child in question wants see a faery, so the spirit will negotiate with whomever is necessary to grant that wish. The faery can be present in human form, in the form of a bird of curious colors, or even in the form of a strange flower that suddenly appears in the middle of a sidewalk, and, wish granted! But if the child does not perform a series of actions to carry it out, such as reading about the faeries in our world or going into a garden or a forest, the wish may not be granted. It is perfoming these actions that pressure the spirit to grant the wish.

Prosperous people are born from a strong collective desire, once many beings have the same feeling connected to a collective desire, a prosperous one is born, and from there it begins to be in charge of granting all possible wishes, sleeping in the hours of the day and working in the dark hours of the night, because the more desires they grant, the more powers and knowledge they receive, and after a hundred years a prosperous person is able to ascend and become a superior spirit of light with much more interesting and complex tasks.

Of course, a person can easily desire something, and after a while forget that desire he had and replace it with something entirely different. Perhaps for the person it is no longer important, but for the spirit or prosperous, these desires are sacred assignments that they must fulfill. They will continue working to grant that wish unless the individual dies, and in this way the spirit is released from their contract. But in the meantime, the spirit will continue evaluating the actions of the individual linked to that desire, even if they are unconscious actions, to grant the desire in question.

LITTLE CALL TO THE PROSPEROUS

Close your eyes and take deep breaths for around 30 seconds, then light a candle in the color that you consider to be associated with your desire (red for love, green for abundance, blue for truth, white for healing, and so forth).

Open your hands with your palms upward and while you focus your eyes on the candle flame, recite three times out loud that desire that you hope will be fulfilled. Do not be afraid to give details about your desire: for/with whom, why, how, when, and where. Let the candle flame burn to the end, nurturing the power of action for your desire.

You can repeat this ritual as many times as you want, and you can also perform it in conjunction with someone else if both are looking for the same desire and for the same purpose.

CALL TO THE PROSPEROUS WITH THE POWER OF THE MOON

On a new moon night, anoint a white candle with camphor or rose essential oil, write your wish twice, first on a piece of paper and second on the outside of the candle using a wooden pin or toothpick. Light the candle and an incense stick and recite the following enchantment:

Oh divine spirits of abundance and wealth,

spirits of desire, fulfillment, and joy

grant this wish that I strongly request this dark night

and just like the moon is nourished by light night after night

thus grows the force that fuels my desire and makes it come true

so my dreams are manifested in my universe

so what today is a wish tomorrow will be a dream come true

and so you, oh divine spirits of abundance and joy

so you will be nourished by the joy and satisfaction of seeing my wish come true.

So be it and so shall it be.

At the end of this enchantment let the candle burn out and keep the paper close to you. From this night, take one minute every night to recite the new enchantment for the next fifteen days until the full moon is formed, so you will nurture your desire with more and more power every night, giving it more and more energy.

AGATHOS DAEMON (ἈΓΑΘΌΣ ΔΑΊΜΩΝ/NOBLE SPIRIT)– THE FAMILIAR SPIRIT

During the early ages of the earth, the old gods (the Titans) gave birth to the first men (the Golden Age). They were subjects of Chronos, the leader of the Titans who ruled with an iron fist during a long period of tyranny. However these men did not age, get sick, or die.

Once this period ended with the arrival of the new gods (the Olympians led by Zeus), these first men were wiped off the face of the earth and Zeus created a new race of men (the silver race) who were bread eaters and wine drinkers, and as beautiful as they were useless, so Zeus eliminated them as well.

A third race arrived (the bronze race) also created by divine decision. These men were born from the fruits of ash trees, ate meat and bread. They were warriors, but they were mortal, and they died with the arrival of the first plague.

Zeus then created a fourth race, also made of bronze, these were more noble, intelligent, and generous, born of the semen of gods in the bellies of mortal women. This race gave birth to heroes and demi-gods like Heracles and Perseus.

After this race, the fifth race of man (the current race) arrived on earth, all descendants of the fourth bronze race, descendants of gods, heroes, and philosophers. But according to myth, due to the impurity in the hearts of these men, they were increasingly cruel, ambitious, treacherous, and unworthy.

Despite all of the above, Zeus lived with this race, the offspring of his children, to ensure that they had a conscience and a greater direct connection with divinity. Zeus took the consciences of all the men who inhabited the Golden Age and turned them into divine spirits, and these *daemons* took care of each human being from just after the moment of birth until their last breath.

The greatest Greek philosophers and scholars saw these daemons as an extension of personal divinity. Homer identified them as protective spirits in charge of leading man toward the fulfillment of his destiny. Hesiod saw them as Zeus's direct connection to men, thus maintaining his role as protector of humanity. Platon supported both ideas, promoting that a daemon was an intermediate spirit between gods and men, an individual magical genie who took care of each man and woman.

One of these guiding spirits was *Agathos Daemon*, an entirely beneficial and divine class spirit who was the grandson of Gaia, the Earth—hence his representation as a spirit of nature—and son of Demeter—hence his divine essence.

This particular daemon only attracted good omens and fortune, good luck, health, and wisdom. He was also capable of manifesting himself in the life of any individual who was deserving, and once he manifested himself in the life of the person, he blessed her with good fortune, success, and wealth.

Like God of Wines and Vineyards
As the following passage quotes, Agathos Daemon was considered by the Greeks a minor deity who cared for the vineyards and other crops.

> In Greek mythology, he is also the [good or noble spirit] of the cereal fields and vineyards. It was the custom of the ancient Greeks to drink a glass of pure (unmixed) wine in his honor at the end of each meal. —Aristophanes, *Equites,* 106

Turned into Angels by Christians
Just as the Greeks had a firm belief in the daemons, so would many other cultures, such as the *Qareen* from Islamic literature, Arda Fravaš in

Zoroastrianism, or Domyo and Dosho in Japanese Buddhism, to name just a few.

This idea of a guiding spirit that is assigned from birth to death is also similar to the concept of the guardian angel of early Judaism, where there was a common idea that each nation, city, or family group would be under the guidance and care of a divine spirit. Later in the 5th century the Christian theologian and philosopher Pseudo-Dionysius the Areopagite made use of these conceptions to promote the idea of guardian angels.

And now we have winged creatures of divine descent who care for each individual The same spirits remain among us, consciously watching over us and guiding our steps, although now in a much more peaceful way.

How to Work with These Gods and Spirits

Have you ever entered your neighbor's house without being invited? Have you answered the phone at two a.m. to find it's a wrong number? Have you organized a party or family gathering and suddenly a stranger you did not invite arrives and makes a lot of noise and asks you for food and favors?

I'm sure you managed to identify with one of these options, and now I'm sure you understand how bad it feels when a stranger knocks on your door wanting something, especially when this stranger hasn't even introduced himself to you. How could this strange character come around asking you for things?

That is the reality that is lived in most religions, spiritual groups, sects, and congregations. It does not mean they are all wrong, it just means that no one has taken the time to explain the basic good manners that they should apply when making a request.

When you decide to join a religious group or venerate a god on your altar or in your home, it is extremely important to show a real interest in the growth and development of your relationship with the corresponding divinity.

The gods know you, the spirits probably know you, too, but don't take it for granted and act like "obviously they know who I am." It's not just about buying a statuette from an online store, lighting some candles on your altar, and waiting for everything to come because you believe you deserve it. The idea of "ask for what you want and it will be granted" has become very popular. The problem with that is it makes us believe that no effort is required.

But the solution is simple: if you want their attention, work for it. The gods, as much as they may love you, have thousands of followers (and non-followers) that they are watching over at all times, and if you want their attention, you should take the time to show some respect and introduce yourself to them. Get to know them; invite them to your home. Don't just assume they know they are welcome. You wouldn't arrive at your best friend's or your mother's without notice. It is not good manners, much less in good taste.

Make room for them in your home. Let them come in. Make room around your altar. Place a glass of water on the altar to cleanse their energy, or serve the spirits a glass of wine when celebrating something so they can to celebrate with you. In Santeria and other currents of Afro-Caribbean mysticism, there is a deeply rooted custom of serving a cup of coffee by the front door every morning to wake up the spirits.

Never act as if you are home alone once you have invited them into your life. They will be present, so keep the space neat and clean, always affirming "this house is never empty, because there are always guests who bring good fortune with them."

Tell them absolutely everything just as you would your best friend. If something is not going properly in your life, if you feel that abundance is not flowing correctly, if your job is no longer the job of your dreams, if you feel you won't have enough money to pay your debts, don't be afraid to stand in front of your altar and ask them for advice, signs, omens, or to please intercede on your behalf in a situation.

Just as the gods of love feed on desire and passion and the gods of war feed on anger and fear, so, too, the gods of lack and poverty feed on your need, while the gods of abundance feed on your satisfaction, your feeling of fullness and completeness, your satisfactorily fulfilled desires, and the joy that these things produce in you.

So, as you continue to ask them for things, also invite them to celebrate with you for the good streaks and thank them for all the events in which they have interceded in one way or another.

Healing Your Relationship with the Gods of Good Fortune

The gods of good fortune, prosperity, wealth, and abundance are many and are willing to help you. They want to see you grow and prosper, so they can feel comfortable and welcome in your life. That is why it is important that you have a good relationship with them.

Every time you repeat, "I am very unlucky," "Fortune never smiles on me," "only bad things happen to me," you are rejecting the goodness and divine presence of these deities, who are probably putting all kinds of opportunities, jobs, contacts, and signals in your way that you may not take advantage of because they are not what you expect.

You can have a lot of money and very good luck, but as long as your life does not have a purpose, you will still feel that you are incomplete. If the gods and angels of good fortune smile on you and give you opportunities, it is you who must work to honor these opportunities, take advantage of them, and give your life a purpose. It is also up to you to dethrone misfortune if you feel it reigning and give the crown to someone else, like yourself.

Be the king of your life, be the one who leads the way to all your dreams and goals, and let abundance, good fortune, and wealth be your advisors and guardians. Ask for signs and do not ignore them when they appear, or you will miss the good fortune these gods and angels work so hard to send you.

Your Power to Summon and the Four Gods You Must Avoid

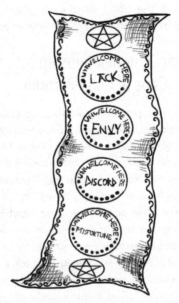

This image represents a small talisman on paper for personal use to keep the four deities, or their manifestations, out of your home. You can draw this image and keep it close to the front door of the home looking outside.

You, as a mage or sorcerer, are a divine manifestation of the universe. You are literally the desire of your ancestors made flesh and blood. Your ancestors asked for the arrival of a hero, a king, or a healer to save their lineage, their lands, and their culture. They prayed for centuries to their gods, and you are the end result of those desires that have finally materialized in this world. As such the load of divine and ancestral power that runs through your veins is enormous, practically unlimited, and infinite.

As a creature of enormous power, your words and actions function as decrees to the universe; everything you think, everything you want, everything you say is charged with enormous power, and it will only be a matter of time before it manifests. One of the differences between the mage and the common person is that the mage knows the origin of this energy and thus takes the best advantage of it. Each spell and each ritual is a whole mathematical equation that is carried out combining the energy of various elements to achieve a particular purpose.

And just as when you call the gods of abundance and good fortune, they will not take long to make themselves present, but there are also four gods that you must be very careful about. The more you think about them or mention them, even unconsciously, the more power you are giving them to be present in your life.

These are the four deities of lack, envy, discord, and misfortune. They are the alter ego of the numerous gods of abundance, good fortune, wealth, and prosperity, and many ancient pagan religions have given names to some of their incarnations.

Just as the gods of war could be considered by many to be undesirable, although, ironically, they were worshiped largely to win the wars of the old days and thus prevent further bloodshed, these four gods, while undesirable, assist all those who have thoughts associated with envy and lack. They feed off people's anxiety, inferiority complexes, and low energy. They are also the ones who assist those sorcerers and magicians who perform magical works to cause misfortune to others, which keeps them quite busy.

At home we call them *the four gods of misfortune* because my mother has a personal belief that they should not be named—not for fear of them, but simply to make it clear that they should not feel welcome in our home. Once you mention them, it is only a matter of time before they will try to implant themselves in your life.

5

CANDLES, CRYSTALS, AND GEMS

When you light a match, or a candle, you are nourishing the world with your own light.

C andles have illuminated the path of man since ancient times. They provide two elements that represent the energy of the sun, heat and light, in the middle of the night, or in cold and closed places, and have been linked to the world of magic and sorcery from its beginning. When combined with crystals and gems, their energy is magnified.

Candle colors are attuned to specific types of energy. Their sizes also vary, usually linked to the amount of power that a ritual carries. For a simple rite, with temporary effects such as an invocation, you would use small, thin traditional candles, while for more elaborate rituals that may be linked to transformation, channeling, or elevation energy with which you want to work, you would use larger candles that can remain lit for many hours or even days.

Candle Magic

Every time a mage lights a match, a flame illuminates the same point in both worlds. Once the wizard unconsciously draws a line from the match to a candle in the air, he is creating a small path of illumination that all the spirits will see in both worlds. And once the magician lights a candle, that small column of wax in a small corner of his altar acts as a tiny lantern of light that illuminates the hidden worlds and thereby illuminates the paths the spirits use to find us. Every time a magician lights a candle, his present desires are marked in fire and light, and this desire will burn illuminating the spirit world until it is completed with their strength.

A Short List of Candles According to Their Colors

WHITE

This color is linked to the moon, and its sacred power to heal arises from the union of all colors, symbolizing purity, sincerity, calm, tranquility, meditation, and spiritual strength.

White candles are used to cleanse and heal the magnetic field (aura) of people, animals, plants, and places. White is the traditional color for candles, and because these candles unite all colors, they can also be used to channel all kinds of energies.

BLACK

This color is under the regency of the planet Saturn. Its power to cut root problems arises from the complete absence of all the colors of the spectrum, which is why it symbolizes darkness and emptiness, the subconscious, and fears of the unknown.

There are a lot of taboos around the use of black candles in magic. They are wrongly associated with black magic and hexes, and it is believed that they can cause harm and misfortune. Their primary use in magic it is to nullify and dispel all kinds of curses and spells, weaken diseases, and reveal things in the subconscious.

YELLOW

This color is associated with Mercury, the messenger of the gods and protector of travelers, and symbolizes earth and joy. These candles are widely used to influence mental activity, creativity, communication, forms of expression, spontaneity, intellect, success in business and wealth—essentially everything having to do with the field of communication and with our ability to relate to others.

Use yellow candles to focus your concentration on a specific objective or bless the owner of a business with good fortune at the decision-making moment. They are also used for rituals before an interview, as their energy will help you be more spontaneous, creative, and sociable.

BLUE

This is one of the colors under Jupiter's rule. The other is violet. It is used to complement all those rituals whose objectives are focused on truth, justice, equity, respect, tolerance, and stability.

Blue candles usually accompany all those rituals to deal with legal matters, to bless, to find and protect documents, and to enhance the

stability of a couple and fidelity. They are also used for spells to achieve greatness, fame, and happiness.

RED

This color is under the regency of Mars, the planet of action and war. It is the color of blood, passion, and fire, and symbolizes vitality, love, virility, sexuality, good health, internal fire, and the realization of personal goals.

Lighting red candles promotes courage, enhances virility in men, activates the nervous system, and protects against envy, bad thoughts, and laziness.

GREEN

This is the color of nature and all its spirits. It is under the regency of Venus, the planet of love, beauty, and desire. It symbolizes fertility, life, honesty, hope and goodness, good luck and fortune, money and abundance. It is the color most used to attract the energy of money and wealth, as well as to unlock our own hidden abilities to bring money our way.

Lighting green candles in the morning before leaving home and thanking the gods of our particular pantheon is a nice daily ritual that I recommend to attract money, progress, and good luck. Green candles are also used to extend the time to pay your bills and avoid indebtedness. A green candle anointed with olive oil that is lit before sunset brings good fortune to the home.

PURPLE/VIOLET

Purple and violet are two different but related colors, very close in the chromatic field with energies that are difficult to differentiate. These colors are associated with emperors and kings, so it is no coincidence that they are under the regency of Jupiter, the Roman god who ruled over the gods. They symbolize faith, spiritual strength, magic, universal consciousness, and transmutation.

Candles of these colors are used to attract fame, recognition, and prestige (though not money), to pass exams and overcome obstacles, to motivate ourselves, or someone else to achieve specific goals, and are also widely used in the New Age culture to transmute energies and perform all kinds of transformation rituals.

ORANGE

The color orange is special in magic and metaphysics: it brings joy, energy, enthusiasm, and creativity. It also brings together the mystical properties of red and yellow as it contains both, so it can be used to attract joy to a relationship or to give us an extra dose of enthusiasm and energy in the midst of a difficult situation.

This color is ruled by the Sun as the King Star and, to a lesser extent, Mercury and Mars. It is an activator of energies par excellence and provides clarity of mind, healing, regeneration, understanding, and happiness.

BROWN

The color of the fertile land, governed by the land itself, is linked to rituals of physical and mental healing, economic stability, fertility, and confidence and also used to restore health, prolong life, strengthen personal relationships, and provide courage and strength to make the correct decisions even when they do not seem so.

Brown candles are best suited to assist in rituals that lead to the physical healing of any illness or to strengthen the body during the application of medical treatment. They are also lit in meditations to strengthen concentration and allow the individual to better channel energy from Mother Earth.

PINK

This is one of the colors ruled by Venus, as is green. It is protective, healing, and beneficial. It combines the magical qualities of red and white; therefore it has a wonderful use in rituals to protect our loved ones, friends, and family members.

Pink candles are commonly used to strengthen a bond of friendship with someone, turn enemies into friends, heal emotional wounds, dispel fears of acting in front of others, fight apathy, raise self-esteem, and attract love and happiness.

GOLD

Depending on the magical tradition this color can be associated with the Sun or Jupiter, although it is mostly associated with the Sun King. For all those rituals that seek to achieve success, money, greatness, fortune, wealth, prosperity, and abundance, this is the color to use.

It is also the correct color to illuminate rituals related to the sun, as well as to channel its light, its heat, and its energy or to attract and channel spiritual guides and gods.

SILVER

This color is completely under the regency of the Moon and the lunar gods and godesses. It is perhaps the color most used by mages and sorcerers who perform magic to contact the moon gods, to attract prophetic dreams, visions of the future, and all kinds of omens, as well as to get superior spiritual help to guide and protect us.

Silver candles are a good complement to light on the nights of the crescent and full moon, as they help us channel the increasing energy of the moon and apply it to our lives.

More Modern Candle Colors

These colors are not as common, but thanks to advances in the science of color, they can be found in candle catalogs, online, and some specialized stores.

MAGENTA

This is one of the most difficult colors to find on the market (but not impossible), a modern color between purple and red that looks like saturated pink. It is linked to the energies of Mars and Venus and an activator of erotic energies. It sensuality, affection, self-confidence, and magnetism.

You can use magenta candles to strengthen a love relationship, promote eroticism within it, or recover lost passion, as well as dispel inhibitions with your partner and stimulate the senses in an intimate way.

CYAN

This is a very light blue-green color, easy to find in aquamarine and turquoise pieces. This color is linked with water and its different phases, more with salty ocean waters than fresh waters. It is under the regency of Neptune, the planet of oceans and their currents.

Candles of this color attract confidence, serenity, and mental strength, but they are also used in rituals to conjure the spirits of the ocean and gods of the sea and make for a more than adequate complement to those rituals for spiritual cleansing that you want to perform on the shores of the sea.

INDIGO

This is an almost violet blue. It has special qualities with regard to the mind. It acts equally on the conscious and the subconscious, represents the innate and psychic magicians of the new generation, and is the color of the candles that you must use to enter in the world of dreams and the astral plane.

This color is ruled in equal measure by Jupiter (the king of the gods and ruler of the heavens) and Neptune (the king of the oceans and ruler of the seas); therefore, it is a color linked to the ethereal elements such as air and water, and also to greatness.

Tips for the Use of Candles in Magic

Store candles together in a cool, clean, dark place. Many believers and witches consider it a bad omen to keep candles in view as if it were something decorative. So unless in a store, there is no reason to display them. They are tools, not decorations.

According to the spiritist tradition and its followers, when making a circle with candles for any ritual purpose, it is advisable to to light the candles clockwise.

There are a lot of taboos around the use of black candles in sorcery, but the truth is that the function of these candles in magic and sorcery is basically to annul and destroy. So yes, although they can be used with bad intentions, they are also suited for performing magical works that seek to nullify spells or curses and dissipate the presence of negative energies in the environment.

Do not blow out candles, except for certain spells and rituals that specify for some symbolic or energetic reason that you extinguish them in this way. Blowing out the candles not only spoils the direction of the energy, it is also related to the bad omen of candles that are blown out by the wind, which indicates a life that is about to leave.

Crystals and Gems for Abundance and Wealth

Agate

This is the stone of good fortune, high vibrations, and health. It also promotes prosperity and a long life, as well as calm, eloquent actions.

Amber (The Gem of Witches)

This resin has the power to balance, and calm the thoughts of those who carry it. It attracts prosperity, luck, and good fortune, especially to those who are dedicated to the magical arts, the study of metaphysics, and the practice of sorcery.

Amethyst (The Stone of Transmutation)

Well known in the metaphysical community for its transmution abilities, this gem evokes the powers of the violet transmuting ray and is essential for every magician's cabinet. It can turn all kinds of negative situations into positive ones. Its use attracts balance, friendship, humility, understanding, and wisdom. It is also very suitable for spells that seek to transmute lack, absence, and need into abundance, understanding, and fulfillment.

Aquamarine

The gem of sailors, mermaids, and sea spirits, it is widely used to prevent drowning and boat accidents. In general, it brings happiness, well-being, peace of mind, and joy to those who carry it with them for long periods of time.

Crystal Quartz

Also known as rock crystal, it stimulates the creation of energy that is used to create new things. It is a receiver, transmitter, and amplifier of all kinds of energy and vibrations of all levels. It is also an incredible cleaner of negative energy. In combination with amethyst it creates a perfect amulet to cleanse, dissipate, and transmute negative energies, and it is the gem that I recommend you use to magnify the powers of your rituals.

Emerald (The Gem of Balance)

Use this gem when you feel you are having problems balancing your time. It helps to focus your mind on your priorities. It helps remove obstacles from your path, prolongs life, and symbolizes abundance. It is widely used in rituals to attract economic prosperity, good fortune, and success in business.

Jade

This stone is used to purify energy and strengthen those rituals associated with prosperity, peace, love, fertility, good luck, longevity, and abundance.

Lapis Lazuli (Special Mention)

Although this stone is not associated with material wealth or abundance, but rather with protection, psychic power, magic, strength, and emotional balance, I think it is a good option to complement your magic in general, in particular your spells to conjure good fortune—especially worn as jewelry.

Pearl

This gem symbolizes purity, innocence, and kindness and is widely used in white magic as a protection amulet. It absorbs negative energy, allows you to calm your thoughts, and attracts longevity and good luck in love, life, and business.

Pink Quartz

To attract good fortune and prosperity it is important to keep your mind focused on what you are wishing and looking for. If you find this a difficult task, rose quartz is right for you. It stimulates the fluidity of positive thoughts and patience to face difficult situations. It is used to treat problems of attachment, loneliness, sadness, anxiety, and anguish.

Pyrite (Fool's Gold)

Because it has a powerful psychic and spiritual vibration, this is the right gem for psychics and mediums. It focuses psychic energy and cleanses and strengthens the aura. Worn as an amulet, it attracts good fortune, money, abundance, good business, and success.

PART TWO

ABUNDANCE, PROSPERITY, AND WEALTH

What old patterns, beliefs, taboos, or judgments come up when I tell you about abundance, prosperity, magic, and manifestation?

6

ABUNDANCE

---

*An energy at your fingertips, a lifestyle, and a force
that moves everything.*

---

*They may brabble for long hours and dark nights about those
taboos they have in relation to money and good fortune, but it is
you who is in the power to decide which of these thoughts and
ideas to listen to, keep, and put into your own practice.*

The word *abundance* comes from the Latin *abundantia*, which
means a large amount of something. The word *something*, being
an indefinite pronoun, includes the full spectrum of things for
which there can be abundance, which is infinite, and includes material and immaterial things. There can be an abundance of knowledge
and wisdom, experiences and beautiful memories, or simple economic
wealth.

Abundance has always been linked to crops and agriculture,
which is logical because the farmer works every day for an abundant
harvest to feed and support his family. But abundance also has a negative side.

If that farmer just sits down and waits for the crops to bear fruit on
their own, constantly compares himself to more succesful farmers, or

any other farmers for any reason, thinking his crop will not be as good, he will feel unmotivated because of those negative thoughts, resulting in an abundance of frustration when he sees those negative thoughts come true. Then merchants will buy from other farmers who offer a better and more abundant product.

While magic and sorcery are a powerful method to help you achieve your goals in the short and long term, your intentions must be in perfect alignment with your purpose in order to achieve the result you expect.

Attention and intention in magic are extremely important; they are intimately linked with the processes of cause and effect. That is why before performing any ritual you must ask yourself clearly and accurately, perhaps even calmly meditating about, what exactly you are looking to achieve with that ritual.

Let's say I am going to perform a ritual to attract love, but is love what I want? Do I just want a sexual relationship, an emotionally strong and stable relationship, or both? Am I prepared for an emotionally stable relationship or was I the emotionally unstable one in my past relationships? Because if so, it would be better to perform a ritual for maturity and recognition of my part in the matter, and after that, another ritual to recognize what exactly I am looking for in a relationship.

Like the case I just raised, the list of questions can be endless, and if your intentions are not clear, the base of your spell won't be either. You may as well perform a spell asking for a car and the next day inherit the car of a relative who coincidently had a tragic death just after you performed the ritual. If you learn anything from performing the rituals that I propose in this book, it is that coincidences do not exist.

When you do not take the time to meditate on the real intention of your magical work, you are simply submerging your body in the river and shaking the water in all directions. That is what you do when you perform one of those quick spells of prosperity, without knowing the exact rational origin of your magical work.

The theme of abundance is more complex than it seems at first glance. Abundance is the natural state of everything that is alive, of everything that moves and of everything that flows. It is the natural state of all things to be abundant and prosper, and working with a constant cleaning of your energy and with the series of magical works you will find in this book, you will be able to re-establish this cycle of flowing energy in your environment and positively manifest everything you are looking for.

We can define abundance in two different ways—the abundance of things (projects, places, memories, dreams, goals, and the like) or as the absence of needs. And though on the surface abundance may look like the lifestyle of someone who has everything, seen in depth it can also be the lifestyle of someone who is not missing anything.

Most importantly, the vision you have of abundance is something that belongs only to you. If your vision of abundance is to have a comfortable apartment, a dog, a healthy life, a stable relationship, and a good job, you must understand that you have to respect that vision. And if your vision of abundance is to live in large mansions and travel constantly, that is your vision and nobody has the right to take it away from you. Once you define your vision for yourself as a person in abundance, you are defining the steps you will take in that direction and the lifestyle you will dedicate yourself to. You will also be defining or sometimes ignoring the lack of something.

Lacking something or living with the absence of something is not precisely something negative. Unfortunately we often associate the term erroneously beyond its meaning: abundance we see as something entirely positive, forgetting that you can also abound in different negative aspects (as we have explained above), while lack is not entirely negative, because you can also lack diseases, you can lack enmity, you can lack financial problems.

The correct thing would be to affirm concretely, once you have solved some problem or some problematic situation, something like "Thanks to the gods and the universe I always have a solution for everything." In this case, the energy is entirely different, because just when you solve a problem, you assume and decree that you are able to deal with this and any other situation. Far beyond modern positive thinking, this is not positivity; this is pure magic in every expression. You are affirming by way of a spell that all situations are under your control, no matter how difficult they are.

The Universe Acts Through Vibes and Repetition

The entire universe is composed of tiny particles of light and darkness, all of them working in a perfect set, dancing among themselves, creating harmonies, vibrating together, and forming together all kinds of gases, elements and metals, stellar dust, dark matter, planets, stars, entire galaxies, and a whole cosmos.

All this vibrating and dancing happens in perfect synchronicity, from the stars that appear in the night sky to the ants walking on the grass. Everything is part of this dancing universe that never stops creating and transforming everything. Absolutely everything. However, not everything in the universe is vibrating on the same frequency. There are very high frequencies capable of colliding titanic fire stars to form new nebulas and galaxies. Everything that is alive and moving vibrates, and the higher its vibration, the higher the frequency it can reach, but there are also other much lower frequencies—frequencies so low and so slow that they are lost in the universe. These low frequencies, are poor by nature, and when the planets and their inhabitants vibrate in this frequency, they freeze, disappear into the dark, and are eventually consumed by some wandering star that devours them like a lion eating a small, tender sheep.

Just as everything in the universe vibrates, these vibrations are also repeated. This happens with the great stars and galaxies and also in the day-to-day lives of human beings.

AN EXERCISE ABOUT OBSTACLES

Close your eyes, take a deep breath, and remember for an instant the last great obstacle you faced. Focus on it for a moment, analyze it, then put it aside and look further back in time. Keep remembering and associating memories, and you will notice that the same obstacle occurred in your life before. Maybe it was a different size or different shape, but it was always the same obstacle, always the same problem you just saw it differently.

I like to call these obstacles *tests*. And if anything has taught us about life, it is that these tests are repeated again and again, not only to strengthen you and constantly remind you that you are capable of doing great things, but also to make you remember that the lesson this obstacle came to teach you is a process of repetition that escapes us.

If a scientist tells you tomorrow that he managed to turn something as simple as a piece of wood into something as complex as a diamond (since a piece of carbon turned into a diamond would not be that interesting), you can be sure that it will only be a matter of years before someone repeats the process and takes it further. If today you stumbled upon a rock on your way to work because you were busy reading the news, even if you move the rock tomorrow, at another time and in another place, you will be distracted again and stumble, not over a dog, or a cat, or a book that someone dropped, but over another rock.

The repetition process is inevitable, but the learning process is not, you can stumble another hundred times over a rock along the way while distracted, but once you learn the lesson and accept that it is not the fault of the rock that is in the way, but you who have always been distracted, you will understand that it is not about stumbling or the rock, it is about not being distracted. When that happens and you learn the lesson, then, you will graciously stumble over something other than a rock.

Vibrations and repetition work together but do not mix. Your vibration is what allows you to move between different frequencies. When your mood is low, your vibration is extremely low, and you vibrate on the same frequency as other minor things. Then you start to feel that way—smaller, tiny, almost invisible, probably sad, and even sleepy and depressed. But if instead, you are in a good mood, you are very lively, cheerful, and feel full of energy, it is because you are vibrating at a much higher frequency, and this will lead you to connect with other projects, entities, places, events, and people who are vibrating at that same frequency. It is a "surround yourself with good and you will be one of them, surround yourself with bad and you will be like them" situation. It is this same principle but applied in a much more practical and personal way.

Do you want to listen to jazz or Latin music? You just have to tune in to that frequency on the radio. But if you want to listen to jazz, and you voluntarily tune in to the hard rock station, you are not going to feel aligned with what you desire. So what do you have to do? Tune in to the correct station. If you want to vibrate in the frequency of money and abundance, you must make a minimum effort and try to tune in to that frequency.

Try complaining less about what you don't have or what bothers you. Try being thankful for what you have, what you have had, and everything that is coming your way. Try being thankful for those doors and roads that have been closed to keep you away from people, destinations, situations, and places that do not correspond to you. Try counting your blessings one by one, and you will vibrate at a different frequency—the frequency of gratitude—and at that frequency, everything you are grateful for returns in triplicate.

Money and abundance never lack

In the house with the yellow flowers.

The Mage's Vibe

Once on a visit to the Amazon in Venezuela, I heard of a group of astrologers who were there as tourists taking selfies and talking. For them, witches were "beings of low frequency," and they believed these beings of low frequency were naturally miserable and, therefore, "always did evil."

I could not disagree more with these people for a number of reasons. The first is that even astrology was a victim of religious and social prejudices at the time. It was prohibited because it was considered "a science of the devil." Even today it is considered immoral by many—just like sorcery, divination, and all forms of magic that someone with prejudice cannot understand.

The second reason is much more personal. It is because I had previously heard that phrase, or a very similar one, in the mouth of someone else with a different perspective. Richard Diaz Hernandez, a renowned Venezuelan spiritualist claimed on television that "the good witches work with the spirits of the light," while "the evil witches work with the spirits of low light and darkness," explaining that the low-light spirits are the souls in sorrow and all those reluctant ghosts that could not go to the other world because they did not receive an appropriate burial, left tasks unfinished, were cruelly murdered, or made deals with dark beings.

But something interesting was happening in Venezuela, where the spiritualist and the witch were not very different. Most of their books and magic manuals are full of rituals and very condensed explanations on how to raise or release the low-light spirits to help them to go up to the highest plane, but none of these manuals told you how to work with them. And if you dared to carry out a search on the Internet (as was my case) or in bookstores on how to work with these *low-light* spirits, you would probably discover nothing, because low-light spirits do not willingly work or agree with anyone voluntarily. Low-light spirits are only mentioned in rituals to scare them away or lift them toward the light.

In my opinion it was more a matter of prejudice than knowledge, especially if you take into account that all books of witchcraft and modern magic, even those that focus on the more traditional aspects of sorcery, are being strongly influenced by astrology, conventional practice, and the phases of the moon. So it did not seem, at least not from the point of view of a sorcerer, that astrologers and witches were so different from each other.

The so-called low light refers to a very low energy vibration frequency that certain types of spirits have, more specifically ghosts and wandering souls. Some of them had painfully tragic deaths or deaths so traumatic that the souls of these individuals still cannot understand what happened or they keep repeating the memory of their death in a kind of trance they cannot escape without the help of a medium or a sorcerer.

This low-light frequency is a slow frequency that these entities move within, and it is difficult for them to move out, while the not yet mentioned *high light* refers to that frequency where spirits of greater power and stronger vibration move. That includes all those elemental spirits, avatars, angel messengers, ascended masters, and gods, all those beings of energy that have the ability to transform the course of things and work all kinds of miracles that influence us positively.

The sorcerers and mages differ from the rest because although many may not know the frequencies that surround them, they know how to move between them and use them in their favor. The sorcerer also has the power to learn to raise his vibration as high as necessary in order to conjure various effects and results to alter different aspects of reality.

On one occasion, trying to understand how these metaphysical issues around frequencies and vibrations worked properly, I asked my mother how she would understand them, and she explained them to me, based on one of the trips we made to some small native town from Venezuela.

She told me, and I quote:

Imagine the natives living in those villages: Many of them may not have access to the same education as a person in the city. Some of them speak little of our language but perfectly speak their own languages. And maybe they don't know how to do equations, but they do know hunting, knitting, sowing, fishing, predicting the weather without the need for many tools, and are able to build a house for their families in just days. They have a clear lack of certain knowledge, but they have a remarkable and even enviable abundance of other knowledge that we lack.

Now remember when you saw them swimming in the river. They are expert swimmers, and they are even able to fish with their own hands and jump from high rocks to the river without receiving any damage. But you who have read a book know what they might not: where the river begins and ends, which other rivers intersect with the road, and what species of fauna and flora you can get in them.

Just like this example, so is the life of sorcerers: Many know the practice but not the theory. Many others focus on the theory but ignore the practice. However, those who are immersed in practice, even if they lack the right books, are capable of working true ritual works of high magic without much problem, since experience, dedication, and constant work has taught them to move between rivers and frequencies without knowing what they are or where they come from. But they do it, and they do it remarkably well.

The frequency of a sorcerer is what differentiates him from the rest of humankind, that the sorcerer is able to open and expand his own energetic vibration to move in different frequencies and, thus, beyond simple magical operations, can enter other worlds—the world of dreams where centuries-old spirits inhabit memories and stories and the astral world where the essences of gods and spirits converge with magicians and alchemists to share their knowledge, waiting for them to deliver it to humanity.

Conjuring Abundance

*Those seven bay leaves in the wallet give more abundance
than the space they take.*

Abundance and prosperity are forces intimately linked to all the energy that surrounds us. Everything you think, mention, decree, or do is linked to a different aspect of abundance.

The difference between magical methods and non-magical exercises that focus on attracting abundance is that those exercises, such as visualization and positive thinking, focus on convincing you that you are abundant and just by knowing it, you attract it. But if it doesn't work for you, they assume it's because you're not practicing it as well as others. Conversely, magical methods work like ropes that allow you to go hunting, understanding that what you are looking for is near you but hidden in front of your eyes, like a rabbit hidden in a bush in your garden. Just thinking about and visualizing that the rabbit is there will not make it enter the house; instead, you must go outside, try to deceive it, attract it, and capture it. Otherwise the rabbit will not leave the bush no matter how much you repeat to yourself every morning in the mirror "there is a rabbit in my house."

The universe has two clear intentions: longevity and expansion. Longevity is a principle of permanence; it is "being here and wanting to stay here." It is the same feeling that parents have about their adult children. No matter how independent their children are, parents will always want to watch over them. Given that all of us are an intimate part of the universe, it is not strange that we also want to remain here; after all, everything that is alive wishes to remain alive. It is only an extension of the universe's desire.

Expansion is what the universe does, consciously or unconsciously. It is constantly filling out. It continues to stretch, to create stars, and all these stars form huge constellations, and within these bright constellations in the midst of darkness, we can find entire galaxies and planets because the universe continues to grow and create infinitely.

Within all this perfect balance of constant creation where the universe does not stop creating and transforming its own work, chaos also continues to inhabit it. We can assume chaos is like those black holes in space devouring everything that has been created—stars, worlds, constellations, galaxies, and eons of history that will never see the light again.

Now let's look at these examples on a smaller scale. Your own day-to-day life is a constant battle between light and darkness, between creating new forms of entertainment and learning, transforming the old into something new (long live retro and vintage), and expanding our knowledge to cover as many topics as possible.

The universe itself is an abundant force, abundant in masses of stars, energy, dark matter, galaxies, metals, gases, and an endless variety of elements that would take days to name, while you are a conscious extension of the universe, a manifestation! The same as the cosmos you inhabit, you are much more than abundant, you are a source of abundance—and you have the opportunity to decide what your abundance includes.

You have a body, bones, blood, skin, and a large number of organs, but most of your body is essentially water. And if we break it down, you will end up becoming star molecules. What else are we, if not inhabitants of a little blue planet that would be seen as one more star from the firmaments of other skies?

A Reflection from the Inside Out

The World is naturally abundant,

the World has everything you needs to fulfill your purpose.

But even so, the World understands your part in something bigger.

You are naturally abundant,

You have all elements and teachings that you need to fulfill the purpose of your incarnation,

But you won't understand until you see you are part of something bigger.

Just like the universe, you are constantly changing and evolving, and also creating and transforming everything you touch, but you are also naturally attracting everything that seems to be the opposite of you—chaos, disorder, lack. You have the opportunity to choose, as if you were on that bridge mentioned in A Visualization Exercise. You have the opportunity to ask yourself, "Do I want to cling to the lack I attract? Or do I want to attract and manifest what I am: an abundant and prosperous being that it is the very manifestation of the abundant universe that I inhabit?"

Magic is nothing more than the tool we use to attract what we want (the energy) and, more importantly, what we wish. Once you start using your magic, it is only a matter of time before abundance begins to flow more frequently in your direction, and that is where you should focus your full attention—on the positive, on the good, on what you need for yourself, for your loved ones, and for your personal development, spiritually and professionally—and leave behind all of what you don't want, allowing it to go its own way.

What you must understand and put into practice is that abundance is something that must not be taken for granted. You cannot simply assume it is waiting for you. Even if it is nearby, you still have to go looking for it. You have to create new ways and forms to attract it, you have to court it, seduce it as if it were that lover you crave. Make the spirit of abundance not only feel comfortable, but also welcome in every moment of your life.

7

PROSPERITY

---

*Smile at the abundance and prosperity once you see it. It won't
take long for it to smile back in ways you can't imagine.*

The term *prosperity* comes from the Latin *prosperitas*, which
means doing well, having good luck, or success.

Prosperity is the favorable course of something that is
undertaken, created, or transformed. It is not something that we
achieve, but rather it is something that we tune in to as we walk along
the path. Although abundance gives us that feeling of satisfaction and
fulfillment, prosperity is the path that leads us to satisfaction, or rather
the set of prosperity-related facts that occur throughout the process.

So prosperity can be visualized as the well-being that you have and
that you have achieved through some means—a job, a path, a change, a
project, a relationship, something new.

Prosperity is a road with channels that come and go in both
directions. While abundance is something more personal, prosperity is
not something seen from outside, but rather perceived in the reflection
of an individual's actions. This channel works in a manner similar to
cause and effect. It is immediate and karmic, meaning that no matter
what you do, it will come back to you at the right time.

Prosperity is a two-way street: you receive, then you give; you give, then you receive. One is the action and the other is the reaction. What you give comes back to you, while what you receive you give to others– as a teacher who teaches what he has learned, a writer who shares what he has read, a tree gives fruits to those who water it, a god who punishes those who lie in his name, a lover who is in the act of giving that love he has received.

Prosperity depends entirely on two things: your actions and your surrender to something bigger than yourself, and yes, you read it perfectly well–your surrender.

Your intentions must always be linked to your actions, but as long as the gods judge you by your true intentions (the force majeure), humanity will judge you by your true actions. Imagine a politician who lies to come to power. His intentions are clear to the gods and the universe, but mankind cannot judge him based on his true intentions, because they are usually unknown. His real actions, however, can be judged–and punished.

You may have the best intentions in the world, but if you lack actions to prove it, that is what you will receive. You will be surrounded by many people with good intentions that are equally unable to take action. On the other hand, if your intentions are good and your actions show it, that is when prosperity is going to reward you, acting through the universe to give back the good you have done.

The surrender is another case. It consists of learning how to yield and knowing when to do it. Nobody can teach you how; it is one of those things that you will simply do when you prepared for it. *Surrender* is a word with negative connotations. In my case, the image of a soldier who surrenders in war immediately jumps into my head, but even though I know that surrender is something different, I cannot erase that image from my mind.

Surrender consists of voluntarily giving in to something. Hardly anyone can force you to surrender in a situation that is beyond your control, but although giving up may mean abandoning this battle, it can also mean giving in to the wisdom of the gods or to love by letting yourself be embraced by it. You can also surrender trying to reason with bigoted people and say, "I've had it up to here; I can't do this any longer." To surrender is to voluntarily say before the universe, "I accept what corresponds to me, I accept with maturity the result of my actions," and be willing to learn from it.

To properly surrender to the universe, you cannot just put aside the pressures you have weighing on your shoulders or social prejudices regarding having a dominant attitude, always acting as if everything is fine or thinking, "if you do not control what is happening it is because you are weak." You must know that you cannot control what happens in your environment, and that is fine. Once you understand this, and the fact that there are forces beyond you, many of them beyond your understanding and control, you begin to mature. If you understand that, it means you are willing to learn more, as well as ask for help. Also, know it's okay to make mistakes, because we learn from them.

The Prosperity of the Mage

Money is but the means to a goal.

Abundance is but the energy that you attract.

What grows in your life, the good and the bad, is what you call for,

that which you are manifesting, it is what you believe the most.

To be prosperous is not to have money or material things. To be prosperous is to have balance in your life. Prosperity is nothing more than a manifestation of your own inner harmony. What differentiates a very poor person from a thriving person is that the poor person is the one who works, gets paid, and spends exactly what he earns, or even strives to spend more, while a person who thrives is the one who works, gets paid, spends, and still has some money left to enjoy and live life.

You can have a lot of money, but if, to earn more money, you cannot make good use of your free time, do not take advantage of your days off, do not share with your family, your partner, your friends, or your loved ones, lack health and reasons to smile, you are not a prosperous person; you are simply a person with a lot of money.

The prosperity of the mage lies in his deep knowledge about the movement and functioning of energy and its use. The greater the mage's knowledge about this energy, the greater his power to manifest his desires for personal and professional growth in the physical world.

A mage understands that everything in the universe depends largely on creative and conservative energies and that everything in our universe is formed by tiny particles of light and energy that dance and vibrate between them. A mage understands the physical body is temporary, living a human experience, and understands that because of this, his enormous power of manifestation, although infinite, is linked to certain invisible laws. A mage doesn't just wish for something and wait for it—he works for it. And it is this serious, constant, and individual work that allows him to transform the physical plane in accordance with his desires of mind and spirit.

The greater his practical knowledge, and the deeper his wisdom and experience, the greater the mage's power to change the course of events, predict the future, and anticipate what the facts will be. But it takes serious, magical work of constant manifestation.

What happens in your life is what you manifest from your previous one. To manifest is the power you possess to attract what you want into your life, and for that, it is important that you know exactly how to handle your energy and thus manifest exactly what you want around you.

The greatness of the magician, beyond understanding events and anticipating them, encompasses the alchemical transformation of what is impossible into something possible. That is what we magicians do.

Working Your Inner Mage

Close your eyes
Inhale the pain of the world
Exhale love and compassion
Inhale the pain of the world

Exhale compassion and intuition

Inhale the pain of the world

Exhale intuition and abundance

Inhale the pain of the world

Exhale abundance and manifestation

Inhale the pain of the world

Exhale manifestation and love for the world.

Because the healing of the world begins within each one of us.

We choose our belief systems. Believe it or not, your whole reality and the way you manifest your personal abundance are a reflection of your belief system. If something is part of your beliefs, then it will be in your life. This is how magic works.

The universe is abundant for everyone; the problem is the beliefs in your mind that make you believe you are not prosperous. As long as you keep repeating "money is bad and corrupts," "it is better to be poor but honest," that is what you will continue to manifest around you.

As is your mind, so is your universe, and that universe you live in is nothing more than a reflection of what you manifest in your mind. It is nothing more than a reflection of the frequency in which you are vibrating.

As long as you continue to complain consciously and unconsciously about the world around you, your reality, your job, the partner you chose, and the academic career you pursued, you will remain unhappy. Not because the reasons for being unhappy are out there, but rather because you are giving all these notions and ideas the power to bother you and corrupt your own happiness.

As long as you keep a job that you don't like or feel comfortable in, without taking the initiative to create or look for a different opportunity, you will remain unhappy because of your own decision to stay there.

It is of vital importance for the mage, and even more so for the initiate in magic, that they maintain a proper focus on what they really want; hence their purpose and intentions must be clear and their focus must be on the purpose and intention behind each ritual being in perfect alignment.

As a mage you must act wisely, understand what you are doing and why you are doing it, and from there, understand the results of your magical work. That is why you must find your focus and meditate before each ritual that you perform, in order to fully understand what result you are looking for, what magic elements you are implementing, and what the real benefit is.

The clearer your intentions, the clearer your energy, and the clearer the results. Do not be afraid to ask for signs from your guiding spirits, the universe, or the gods and angels that make up your pantheon. Guides and a second opinion should always be heard—not always taken into account, but definitely heard.

6

Richness or Sacred Wealth

Where it is quality and not quantity that matters.

Money is NOT hard to come by . . .

Thinking otherwise is what blocks its energy in your life.

If you keep that line of thought, you will block abundance

from manifesting in your life.

The terms *richness* and *wealth* are used to refer to possession of innumerable resources and tangible and intangible assets. It is the absolute opposite of poverty and should consist in the quality of the things that are possessed, rather than the quantity. While poverty is the lack of necessary things, having richness or wealth is the abundance of the positive, such as money, goods, business, or power, or as I like to count them daily, the abundance of blessings.

Monetary wealth does not make happiness, but it is a symbol of power, well-being, and fullness. Wealth is many times, a physical reflection of your personal inner resources, your abundance of knowledge, wisdom, and experience, or your inner peace.

Wealth refers more to the material goods we possess, to the quality of them, to the quality of your lifestyle from your own perspective, and to financial well-being, without focusing so much on "all the things you have" but rather on all the things that you don't need and that's why you don't have them.

When you are financially independent, the way money functions in your life is determined by you, and not by your circumstances.

—Joe Dominguez, *Your Money or Your Life*

Maybe you don't have a gold necklace, but do you really need that necklace to be happy, prosperous, and healthy? Maybe you only have one vehicle, but do you really need more than one vehicle for your daily tasks? You probably do not have a sculpture by Michelangelo or Da Vinci in the main hall of the east wing of your mansion on a private island, but is it so necessary for you to live on an island away from civilization, in a mansion full of empty rooms whose most interesting company might be a statue that you can't even touch? Do you really need all this to be happy?

Of course, we must not compare happiness with wealth, much less fall into those old empty prejudices that equate money with evil. Money is nothing more than a manifestation of your richness and your inner abundance, and it is up to you to put it to good use or not. Whether you are good or not depends on you, not money, and just as the moral sense of money is not associated with your own morals, wealth and happiness are not associated either.

Some people with a good heart are very happy with very little, while others, unfortunately, need a lot to be happy or to believe that they are. Happiness depends on you, as well as your richness, not money, because having much is not the important thing; the important thing is that you do not lack what you need, be it material or immaterial.

About this, the famous Kabbalist author and lecturer Yehuda Berg once said: "Money is energy and as all energy the more you have, the better. But energy, like the sun, comes with a warning label."

Abundance is the recognition of what is present in high amounts in our environment, be it an abundance of love money, health, or conflicts and obstacles. Prosperity is the positive form of abundance, it happens when we succeed in our projects, when we strive continuously for success, when what we want has become reality and has manifested in a way that is beneficial for us. Richness and wealth are having on hand everything you might need just when you need it, from money to pay bills, to a space to live and create.

Good Fortune–An Introduction to Luck

You are abundant in Love.

You are abundant in Health.

You are abundant in Consciousness.

You are abundant in Compassion.

You are abundant in Wisdom.

You are abundant in Opportunities.

You are abundant in Light and Peace.

You are abundant in Blessings

You are abundant in Joys

You are abundant in Prosperity and Fortune.

Good Fortune is always on your side.

Fortune works like luck and chance, it depends on many factors around you that you probably ignore. It is important that you understand what luck is, because in the end, good fortune is nothing more than a series of acts guided by good luck that manifest in our path.

Luck

Luck can depend on many different factors, from the date and time of birth (astrology) to the numbers and patterns linked to facts or events (numerology and feng shui), but generally it is the positive or negative way in which the results of something we do are manifested, depending on the various factors.

While you make your own destiny, it is also fair to repeat that old saying, "The die is cast," which, although true, only refers to a general pattern of events. Whether luck is in your favor or against you, it does not mean you should take it that way. Luck is either an ocean or a swamp, you are the one who decides if you want to swim in it or move on.

Good Luck

From birth, a series of patterns are written in our environment. Our parents decide our names, clothing color, what to feed us, and which

schools we attend. From birth, the stars are also writing patterns around us, and those patterns will manifest as events and causations in the course of our lives.

When we say a person is born under a good star, it means that the stars were located in a truly beneficial position at the time of her birth, and she will be enterprising and creative,

with energy that will lead her to create and manifest a great abundance in the course of her life, obviously with due effort.

Good luck encompasses the events that flow in our favor, for our benefit. When everything seems to flow positively, good luck is as present as a star that illuminates the path.

Bad Luck

Bad luck, unlike good luck, happens when at the time of a person's birth the stars show catastrophic or unusual events, such as a coup d'etat, an earthquake, an end to a political aspect of a nation. People who are born during these events or during the forecast of them come

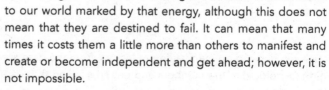

to our world marked by that energy, although this does not mean that they are destined to fail. It can mean that many times it costs them a little more than others to manifest and create or become independent and get ahead; however, it is not impossible.

When circumstances do not flow in our favor, when everything seems to be momentarily blocked, those are the moments where the energy is not flowing correctly. It is there that the term "bad luck" comes in, as a manifestation of this energy.

Nothing is more powerful in the Universe than a Sorcerer, once he has discovered two things—the infinite power he has to change everything and self-confidence.

9
Mages, Sorcerers, and Witches—Where Is the Money?

Breathe slow and deep.

Close the book for a moment.

Close your eyes for a moment.

Visualize that golden light that emanates from you and everything around you.

Visualize those lines of light that connect you with everything around you.

Take a deep breath again.

Open your eyes again.

Open the book and return to this page.

Congratulations, all your paths have been unlocked, the doors have been opened, those obstacles that seemed gigantic have been cleared.

The Complicated Relationship Between Magic and Money

Magic will never make you a millionaire, but it will give you what you need to live.

That line and many of its variants are easy to find in books of magic and sorcery, but it is a truth that you must be very careful with (so maybe take it with a grain of salt).

Magic is a source many people resort to in search of abundance and wealth, and that is not bad. The simple problem that most miss is that we do not seek abundance from the certainty that abundance is our right, rather we search for it from a sense of lack due to the fear of missing out, debts, or ignorance of the subject.

If all the matter in our universe is created from tiny molecules of light and energy, and magic is the way that gods and men make use of this energy in different ways, it is not hard to believe that your personal economy works that way too. From bills and coins to checks and credit cards, money is a form of energy that is subject to the laws of balance and exchange. Universal law (similar to karma) indicates that everything you have you paid for in one way or another. All causes lead to a consequence; all actions have a corresponding reaction; and everything you give or receive is returned or given back.

Money is a physical manifestation of your inner abundance, as simple as it is powerful. The larger your inner abundance, the greater its manifestation. It's not about how much money you have left over, it's about how much more you can get from the resources you have at your fingertips, and that it meets your needs, as well as your pleasures. If that is within your reach, you are manifesting it correctly.

Simply put, money is not static. If you accept this one universal principle, that money flows, you are on your way to understanding wealth accumulation.

—Janine Bolon, *Money Is Not Just For Rich People*

Mages and sorcerers make consistent use of spells, rituals, baths, and amulets to conjure good fortune, success, prosperity, abundance, wealth, and material well-being—also to attract love and joy, strengthen health, provide protection to a place or individual, and even to fight disease or reduce its symptoms. All of this is fine, but once you clarify your intention about what you are trying to attract, you can focus on it in a positive way and give it time to manifest.

The serious mistake that many individuals make in this practice— and I include myself because for many years I was a victim of this same mistake—is that when performing spells to improve the economic aspects of our life, we do it from necessity and ignorance, not from abundance, and therefore we end up canceling our own energy to attract, because we are so often calling the light from inside a dark cave.

You can perform all the spells in the books about "All the Money Spells You'll Ever Need" or "This Year's Best Money Rituals," but as long as you do it with thoughts of poverty and need like "I hope this spell works because my debts keep increasing," or "I hope I never lack money because I have a lot of bills to pay," the same will continue to happen. Those spells are still working perfectly, and they are granting you exactly what you are wanting with your words. Let's analyze them:

"Hopefully this spell will work" (You are taking away power by assuming it might not work.)

"I keep adding to my debts." (You are decreeing in front of your spell that these debts should continue to appear.)

". . . that money never fails me" (Wouldn't it be better "that prosperity never fails me?")

"I have a lot to pay." (You said that you need the money, not to live well, but to pay more debts.)

You are simply getting what you wished for.

It is not just lighting candles to illuminate the path of abundance and burning incense to clear our path against bad energies, successful spellwork is to proclaim and understand that prosperity is part of us, part of you as an individual, and to use incense to cleanse and dissipate those obstacles that are not letting economic prosperity flow in your direction.

Once you understand this and perform those same spells, not from necessity or poverty, but from a feeling of abundance and wealth, those spells will work in a much more beneficial way.

AN EXERCISE TO REMEMBER YOUR ABUNDANCE

Every time something good happens in your life, every achievement, every joy, every celebration, let it flow and memorize how it feels. Once you have memorized it, embraced it, and you will have filed it in your brain and in your soul and enriched yourself with this emotion.

Use that memory to manifest your abundance; remember it and project it constantly—especially while you perform these rituals. In that way they will be driven from love, joy, the festive spirit, so your energy will work with your emotions in a conscious way to try to repeat in triplicate that positive emotion.

Many mages and witches dedicate themselves entirely to studying and developing the most complex spells to attract money, and many times they work. They may not fail, but without the correct process they may attract the money needed, but also more debts and commitments.

Just as mages attract abundance for themselves, they often give others the most wonderful recipes and magical methods to attract abundance. The problem is that these clients or magic students do not understand that this abundance is in some way blocked and you must unblock it before you can invite it in and hug it to you. So they end up performing spells that can be quite superficial, because they only focus on attracting the minimum amount of money needed that also brings more debt.

Another serious mistake is to work with the energy of others before you have worked with your own energy. Performing rituals to attract abundance, wealth, and prosperity for others, in this case, will not attract prosperity to others; it will just spread your own low energy and feeling of personal dissatisfaction. Until you become an abundant person, you cannot help others.

When you perform these rituals and spells from the understanding of abundance, from the understanding of prosperity, from the memory of satisfaction, these rituals gain greater power, because they stop acting as pain relievers and focus on the root of the problem.

The trick here is to focus on the energy within, the energy that you are bringing to the ritual and the direction you are giving this energy, in the power that dwells in the symbols, and in every aspect of the ritual. It is not the color; it is what that color reminds you of. It is not oil; it is what it attracts and makes you feel. It's not about knowing it; it's about feeling it and understanding it.

The true magic is not in the ritual that is performed or in the lunar phases, it is in the hands of the of the magician who knows the work.

Once you begin to perform these rituals for money and abundance from a place of self-love and prosperity, feelings of joy, with sufficient understanding to differentiate what is a need and what is satisfaction, you will have very beneficial results.

When you are a sorcerer who dominates the powerful energy of abundance, it is only a matter of time before all those around you become abundant and prosperous as well.

May that which you manifest, benefit you and all your loved ones.

Just like Lord Ganesha, who embodies the wisdom and compassion of the world, just when the world needs it most.

Here is a little story about why I choose to use pink candles for calling money, and not green like everybody else.

For years my family was struggling with money. Being a family of witches and healers, this was very ironic, but although my mother constantly repeated that at home we were never lacking, food, spirits, and light and this was all very true, the reality is it was not easy to grow up in a small house with only two rooms, with your parents, five sisters, and a huge altar in the kitchen, where we had more flowers on the altar than food in the fridge.

During the same years, quick formulas to make money were constant. We filled entire notebooks with practical spells for just that. Many of them worked perfectly well. It was easy to identify the signs that a spell was it working or not.

But just as the money came, the money went. Mom always repeated aloud to the spirits "bring me customers," and the customers came. They came by the dozen, but most paid with food or used clothing or even offered services such as cleaning the house or repairing the TV, all in exchange for my mother doing a cleaning and me doing a little consultation for them.

All the time we were dealing with this situation, we used green candles, rosemary oil, flowery water–the typical tricks–over and over again. On a certain occasion my mother bought a box of one hundred green candles to perform a one-hundred-day ritual to attract money, decorated and perfumed all the candles with myrrh and sandalwood oil with ashes of sage and powdered palo santo, and lit one every day.

It was little more than three months when so many clients came to the house that I had to miss school to help them, my sisters intermittently stayed or took the day off, and on many occasions the clients stayed to sleep on the sofa to wait until the next morning.

But just as clients arrived, and many of them paid very well for the magical services that were offered at home, after four months this good streak ended, the flow of money resumed its usual inconstancy, and my mother was fed up with the whole situation.

One day as I sat with her to look for a good spell, I noticed that some words in that book were incorrectly translated from English to Portuguese, some misprint, when in Venezuela we do not speak

Portuguese, even where I lived at that time in Rio Black, so close to the Brazilian border that I could practically move there in a matter of hours.

I then checked the information in the book, discovering that it had been translated from a book originally in English published around 1998.

All the author's spells wrapped green candles, and I was always thinking that green was used to symbolize the abundant wealth in the leaves of the trees. To my surprise, reading other books by the same author, I found that the color green was used for money, because it was associated with the most popular bill of all: the dollar.

Understanding this reminded me of one of those conversations about magic and spirits that mom usually has in the kitchen with her friends or with my aunts, drinking coffee and eating cookies, constantly mentioning some terms that I did not know, such as "Americanized magic," "old magic," or "old sorcery."

And I remembered one of those conversations where one of my aunts mentioned, "the dollar is what moves the world, it is not the most expensive ticket, but it is certainly the most important."

Here, I understood that all this time we had been focused on performing spells that conjured money from the perspective of an American author. We were forcing an energy that did not correspond to us. But hey! We were the lucky ones; many people perform these spells and rituals without a proper understanding of them and never know why they do not see results.

So then we made a small change of mindset and began to create our own spells based on what we knew how to do. We replaced the oil of myrrh and rosemary with palo santo (one of the most expensive essences in the country), the green candles for pink and lilac (the colors of the highest denomination banknotes in our country), the jade incense (associated with good fortune) with musk and rose incense, to symbolize elegance, purchasing power, and abundance.

And since then we have spent years working on this, exploring sorcery and being willing to question our rituals from their origins, not because others are wrong, but because not all rituals are made to be used by everyone.

Your First Ritual

Clean first, to conjure later.

Phase I

UNDERSTANDING THE COMPLICATED RELATIONSHIP YOU HAVE WITH MONEY AND ABUNDANCE

Money is bad and having it makes you less humble and much less kind.

Money is pure evil.

Wealthy people are not happy and they don't have any friends.

Those who have a lot of money have nothing else in life.

Money is from the devil and that's why it's better to have less.

Wash your hands after touching money, because it is toxic.

Good people don't have money.

Better to be poor, than be rich and cruel.

The above are some of the hundreds of prejudices that exist around the issue of money, and they could not be more wrong. Life has allowed me to personally meet people with a full abundance of truly happy and very kind economic resources. I've also known people who, without having abundance in their lives, take the easy path that leads them to be considered evil or cruel. Yes, there are many ill-intentioned people out there who have huge bank accounts and manage money that is stained. But there are also many people out there who have worked hard for many years to get what they have without ever having bad intentions in their head, thus demonstrating that the money-happiness relationship is not real. Some are happy with much and others with very little.

What for you is a simple reusable glass, many times for a small child is the funniest of all toys, regardless of the price, because the child is thinking about fullness, not quantity, not prejudice, not what others think. He is just thinking about what makes him happy.

Money is loaded with prejudices, mostly negative, but we forget that money is also used to pay for medicines, treatments for a child with cancer, food, clothing, and housing, and all the luxuries you have, from your cell phone plan and Internet to special winter boots and holiday gifts for your loved ones.

Your relationship with money is nothing more than a reflection of all your other relationships. Just as you treat other people in your life, for example, your work colleagues, they will develop an opinion of you and treat you accordingly. Your relationship with money is no different. It is your decision whether this relationship is love-hate, mutual love, or mutual hate, and how you treat money—as a sacred manifestation of your own wealth or an evil spirit that you don't want close—is how it will treat you.

Until you heal your relationship with money, money will not heal its relationship with you. As long as you force yourself to think that money is something you can live without, while ignoring the fact that it is the very necessity that moves the world, money will continue to treat you the same way: as a necessary entity that does not require you to have it in your hands.

Phase II

HEALING AND APPRECIATION RITUAL IN TWO STEPS

You will need:

- » Three sheets of paper

- » Pens of different colors

- » Yellow and green candles

- » Cinnamon incense

- » A saucer or cauldron

- » A glass of water, juice, wine, or beverage of your choice

Step I—Separate to Understand

Light a yellow candle, a green candle, and the incense, then start the ritual.

Take two sheets of paper and two pens with ink of different colors. On one sheet of paper write (preferably with green or blue ink) your full name in large letters, and below, a full list of everything that you think money is: good, bad, and all your thoughts in general. Now, on the other sheet of paper, you will write at the top (preferably with red or purple ink) "What others have taught me about money," and there you will list, everything that other people—relatives, colleagues, teachers, loved ones, and friends—have made you think about money. No thought is too complicated or too simple to be included.

Next, read each list aloud twice in order to understand what you really think about money and what others think about it that they have inevitably put in your head, so you will understand the good aspects and the bad aspects in a more subtle and fair way and will know exactly where your every prejudice and thought about money comes from.

Finally, burn both sheets in a saucer or cauldron with the flame of the yellow candle. It has already become clear what you think and you have already properly separated your thoughts from the thoughts of others, and by burning it, you have sent a clear message to the spirits of the other plane that you are willing to heal this complicated relationship.

Step II—The Appreciation Act

On a blank sheet of paper you will draw twenty-one lines, and on these write the following:

- » Seven reasons why money was necessary in your past (for example, money paid for my food and my studies)

» Seven reasons why money is necessary in your life right now (for example, rent, Skype to communicate with my family, heat in winter, pay for my children's school)

» Seven reasons why money is a necessary asset for you in the future, yes!

You are not allowed to delete or edit, you must be honest and write what came to your mind at that moment.

The next thing you are going to do is write on the back of the sheet "Thank you, for allowing me all of this and being there at all times, thank you." You will write this as many times as you consider necessary, and at the end of the sheet you will sign it with your name. Roll the paper and burn it in the flame of the green candle.

Keep the ashes of the paper in the saucer or cauldron until the candles are completely consumed and then throw all the remains of this ritual in the trash. From now on you are starting a new life with a new, clearer perspective.

Healing Your Relationship with Money

Material and spiritual wealth, a two-way relationship that you should heal.

Material wealth is no more than a reflection of your own nonmaterial wealth, your spiritual wealth, your intellectual wealth, your emotional wealth: your cultural wealth. All this will manifest in the environment you inhabit, and therefore it is extremely important to maintain a positive relationship with money and everything good and positive that it symbolizes for you.

As we grow up, we receive knowledge and tools that we will use in adulthood. During that process it is inevitable that the same people who are teaching us unconsciously make the mistake of not teaching us to see beyond what they have taught. Because of that, many times we grow up with negative ideas about our relationship with money. After all, our parents have taught us two important things regarding material wealth: First, how good it is to have the things you have instead of living without them, and second, material wealth feeds the ego and is not good. So you must work hard for what you have and also you should not have it because it is bad, both at the same time.

It is a thought as contradictory as it is wrong, not to mention that it is inane to think you cannot cling to material things because they are not important while at the same time thinking material things will stunt your growth. But hey! Didn't you just tell me that material things are not important? But they can stop my personal growth? That is important! Don't you think?

Untangling the Four Essential Concepts

In order to sort out the confusion, we must define four concepts we have spoken about that go hand in hand and are often confused with each other: abundance, wealth, money, and superficial materialism.

While abundance is based on the amount of necessary things you have (quite the opposite of lack), wealth is based on the quality of these things. Cultural abundance (a person or country that has a huge appreciation of its cultural diversity) is very different than cultural wealth (a country with a huge culture of its own that deserves to be explored and appreciated). Likewise, an abundant plate of food is not the same as a plate of rich food; there is the difference of quantity vs. quality.

Money is the means that allows us to acquire either abundance or wealth. Whether you invest your money in the best car of the year or in several cheaper cars, the money is there in the middle. It is simply the means of exchange that is used, like the Old Ones exchanged grains for rice or chickens for vegetables. Money, in any of its current representations, is only the natural evolution of this intermediary in the process; it is what defines the value of the transaction and allows its action.

Given all this, materialism—the conduct and superficial attitude that surrounds everything that is associated with money—is what few mention but all unconsciously confuse, and in that way we create an involuntary association between abundance and materialism, wealth and materialism, money and materialism, and end up seeing everything under the same lens.

All this prejudice surrounding money is something complex and difficult to ignore. It is common today that even the youngest want to have access to the best smartphone on the market or the best vehicle, because the new generations have moved away from their traditions and cultures associated with money, old social prejudices, and more classic ways of thinking. Praise be to all the gods of science and evolution for that reason.

For new generations a car is more of a work tool that saves them time getting to the office than a social tool, as it used to be in the 1970s and '80s. Same with smartphones, that in their early years were something reserved for a fairly exclusive public and only the wealthiest could afford and maintain, but these have now become a practical tool for social relations, communication, and work. The most enterprising young people use these devices to read the news, listen to music, watch movies, share files and work folders, hold conferences and video calls with their families and colleagues, and even, as in my case, to write a book.

Perhaps that is why the new generations have a clearer vision of the world that many members of past generation have a hard time understanding, because they lack the same prejudices with which you and I were raised. They also see money as what it is: not as a luxury, not as something exclusive, but the tool you need to pay for the things you need, more as an ally than an enemy, contrary to the vision we had about it in previous generations.

If, like our older generations, you look at money as an enemy, as something that is hard to get, as something foreign to you and you constantly repeat to yourself, "I need it and I don't have it," you can be sure it will stay that way.

A LITTLE RITUAL TO CLEANSE THESE THOUGHTS

This brief ritual is a task that I like to entrust to all my readers and my students, especially those who attend my workshops and online classes on **Abundance Magic.**

It consists of taking a simple sheet of paper, and writing twenty-one things that you think you know about money on one side of the paper and then writing twenty-one things that you think you know about magic on the other side.

Next to each of these concepts, you are going to write down the origin of that belief. For example: "money is bad and corrupts," "because that is what my parents taught me," or "money is good and it helps," "that was what my ex-girlfriend told me."

This work will help you analyze those beliefs you have about money and their origin. It will also make you question many of these beliefs that you still have in your head, because that pattern you are forming in your head, that mindset you have about magic and money, has power over all the spells and rituals you perform.

HEALING YOUR PERSONAL RELATIONSHIP, FAMILY KARMA, AND FAMILY TREE WITH REGARD TO MONEY

It is not an easy task, but with constant work you will achieve it. I recommend you perform this simple ritual at each new moon of the month, and yes, I recommend being consistant with it and doing it for several months in a row. Light a white candle and say the next words aloud.

Here I understand and from here I return your relationship of scarcity, lack, and limitation against money. These thoughts and understanding do not belong to me, so with all the love in my heart and with deep appreciation and respect, I return them to you. With infinite love and with infinite gratitude, do with these thoughts and prejudices what you want, but I forbid you to return them to my life, my mind, and my heart. Here I understand

and from here and now I am creating a new relationship with money, wealth, abundance, and generosity, that just as I receive everything I want and get everything good that I seek and need, so can I also give to others, because I can and because it is easy to do, because from this moment I break that limited understanding that you had about money and wealth. And from here my relationship and the relationship of all who come after me are healed, are mended, are purified, and are loaded with abundance and wealth, so be it.

Moving from Study to Practice

With your vision and conscience you drive it away,
but you also attract it.

Now that you understand the deep-rooted beliefs that you have about money, it is time to go from theory to practice. You have already learned to add, so now let's move on to the equations.

Magic and sorcery are two parts of the same holistic science. While energy is that which emanates from everything that exists, whether it is alive or not, magic is the principle of action that moves energy by redirecting it or transforming it to create a change in the environment.

Magic is the consistent study of this energy, and sorcery is the practice of what you have learned from those studies. You can dedicate yourself to studying energy and the way magic works, but it is simply not useful if you don't practice it. You neither help others with your knowledge, nor receive profit from it (the economic wealth that is present in the form of payment).

Now as a sorcerer, you must go into practice and work on your relationship with this energy and the healing of it. Perhaps you will not become a millionaire in the process, but listen to me when I tell you that your life will change in incredible ways.

In this book you will find a combination of formulas to work this energy as well as to say goodbye to your visions of scarcity, because scarcity as such only lives in your way of thinking and understanding your environment. What many see as a risk, creatives see as inspiration, and entrepreneurs as opportunity. What the wealthy and businessmen see as a simple hammer is a source of income for the blacksmith. And what for one person with no vision of the future seems like a person who works too much for nothing, for the one who works it is the material sustenance of his family. Those arduous hours of work become money, and money ends up being translated into food on the table, vacations to beautiful places with loved ones, and medicines for old age, because often the shortages are more a matter of perspective than reality.

Your relationship with money is more important than you think, because you are inhabiting a body of flesh and blood on a material plane, and the sustenance here is material, which is why the sooner you heal this relationship with your money energy, the sooner you can begin to manifest a better life.

The Art of Letting Go

Something that many New Age authors teach is that every time you perform some kind of spell or ritual that affects someone else's will (a love spell for example), you are misusing your energy, and it is considered black magic by the most extreme. Many of them also consider casting a spell on someone else, even if this spell or ritual is not directly connected to their will (for example, a spell of protection or good luck), you are also breaking certain unwritten laws and are again considered a dark magician for imposing your will on the lives of others.

But the truth is, in magic we work with intentions, action, and purpose. If your intentions are good toward someone else, if your actions (the spell in this case) have a positive objective for that person (for example, a remote healing spell for someone who is recovering from surgery), and you do not want any recognition, just to help this person in this difficult situation, do you think it is improper or immoral and should not be done? In the end, every time sorcerers carry out a ritual, are we not imposing our will in some way on the designs of nature, gods, and destiny?

A Lesson I Learned by Watching

This is a personal anecdote. My mother is a well-known Healer/Santera, a kind of very eclectic seer and witch with many followers who seek her help and advice. She has a remarkably strong character, even easy to fear, but behind that strong character, she is a person who helps others often without expecting anything in return.

My mother is the kind of person who is always attentive to others, although she often does not admit it. She is also the kind of person who likes to know everyone's problems, but not out of morbidity; on the contrary, she listens to everyone's complaints about their problems and always responds with a very serious "you have to put character (be brave and strong, keep firm) to see how you can fix that, things do not fix themselves." When people come to ask for spiritual help, many times she focuses on carrying out her work (a spiritual cleansing of a house or a vehicle, a healing, or other work). And in general people end up trusting her so much that they tell her about all the other problems they have in their love life or family, and she always pretends not to listen to them.

But at the end of the night, when she gets home tired from so much work, she prepares her food, sits down to eat while reading some text, and after that, she puts on her white hat, lights some candles on the altar next to the kitchen, lights a cigarette, and begins to pray to the Orixas and the Great Spirit, for example, to help "Senora Marta's son," who is doing very poorly in his studies, and asks for conscience and mental clarity for him, or to pray for "the sister of the neighbor whose name I forgot to write down," so that the spirits give her the strength she needs to overcome this terrible divorce without problems. Or there was the occasion when she was awake until dawn, praying for "the daughter of a colleague from the university," asking that the Great Spirit help her find the necessary will to abandon the world of drugs that she was having such a hard time leaving.

So I learned something very important—actions in front of others are powerful, but it is those actions and good intentions done from the heart, those that you keep secret, that really show your true colors.

Blessing Others with Abundance

Do good without looking at who.

When you plant the seed, the seed already knows what it is,
and that will not change.
The seed already knows what type of tree, bush, flower, or herb it is,
and that will not change.

Since you came to this world, you are naturally abundant;
your environment has convinced you otherwise, with fear and
prejudice.
It is time for you to recognize who and what you are.

You are human,
you are spiritual,
you are wise,
you are kind,
you are abundant,
you are magical,
you are a divine inspiration,
you are the embodiment of the desire of your ancestors,
you are the light at the end of the tunnel for many who lean on
you.

Many times when you are aware of a problem, you do not realize that the solution others are looking for is you, and it is your magic that can resolve it. Many people do not ask for help, either because they are embarrassed or afraid of being judged based on the situation, but if you feel any kind of appreciation for these people and you can do so, my recommendation is that you volunteer your help.

Regardless of whether you decide to help people or not, regardless of whether or not you want to, regardless of whether you dedicate yourself to working with magic and this is your profession or simply a hobby for you, regardless of all this, here I leave you a brief ritual to bless someone else's life with abundance and serenity.

All the good that you do for others finds incredible and wonderful ways and means to manifest itself back to you, whether others know the good you did or not, whether others appreciate it or not.

THE RITUAL OF BLESSING SOMEONE ELSE WITH ABUNDANCE

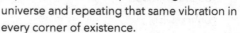

Abundance is a natural blessing, and every time you help someone else, every time you are kind to someone else, every time you perform an act of goodwill for someone else, that frequency in which you are vibrating, those waves you produce, will end up travelling across the

universe and repeating that same vibration in every corner of existence.

I invite you to bless someone else—a colleague, a loved one—with this little ritual of prosperity, and no, do not worry about letting them know. One of the most beautiful feelings you can experience is the sensation of seeing with your own eyes and knowing that you did somebody else good and see good things happening to them along the way.

Before carrying out the following ritual is important to know something: You are not imposing your energy on someone else's life, you are neither negatively influencing the will of these people, nor are you forcing them to do something they do not want to do. You are simply shedding a bit of clarity on their path, attracting prosperity, wealth, and the chance that their good wishes will find a way to be fulfilled.

Ritual

On a Thursday, a day ruled by Jupiter, using gold ink write down the names of seven people that you want to bless with clarity and good fortune. Choose these people according to your good intuition and logic, don't just bless people because it will be good for you or because you want to look good to them.

Here you have the opportunity to help those people that you really think may need it or that would benifit them at this time, and to do that, write three reasons why this person requires this blessing under each name, for example:

> » "Aranza is a wonderful person who is always willing to help others without asking for anything in return."

> » "Julian helped me a long time ago when no one else did and since then I have been grateful to him."

> » "Alex has had a difficult life, but now he is finally restructuring his life in the right way and I hope this will help him to make his best decisions."

Light a mint or eucalyptus incense stick, one green and one red candle, then anoint your hands with a mixture of lavender and rosemary essential oil. Take the paper between both hands, and recite the following enchantment:

Seven names, seven lives, seven souls that I bless tonight.

Seven names, seven lives, seven individuals that I bless tonight.

Seven names, seven lives, seven minds that I bless tonight.

Now moisten the paper completely with your hands and roll it like a parchment. Tie the parchment with green and gold thread, and while reciting the following enchantment, burn the paper roll in the candle flame. Recite:

O great gods and spirits who watch over the well-being of every soul whose name is written,

Oh great gods and well-meaning spirits who hear my prayers tonight,

O great gods and spirits who bring clarity, love, generosity, abundance, and goodness,

To all of you I venerate tonight, this smoke and its perfume is yours, this light before me is yours, and tonight it is yours, therefore in return I ask that you bless these seven names without any doubt, that each of them will get that growth you are looking for, love, light, and abundance, with that I bless you, clarity, generosity, and goodness, with that I bless you, work for the well-being of all of them and in every aspect, and without expecting anything else in return, I hope. May they all be here and every night be blessed.

So be it, thanks!

The remaining ashes of this spell can be mixed with soil and flower seeds and buried in a nearby patio or garden.

The problem is you think of money as a foreign entity that you only receive to deliver immediately.

The solution is looking at money as it really is, a physical manifestation of your inner wealth, a divine expression of your abundance.

Money is an instrument that is in your hands to achieve something else, money is not the end itself nor is it the goal, do not be wrong with it.

PART THREE

DESIRES, WISHES, AND SPELLS

Mages work on what they want, working the magic of desires.

That which you are seeking to manifest in your new reality,

also has a deep desire to manifest in your current reality.

You have the power to manifest everything you want,

you just have to believe it and take responsibility for those beliefs.

10

DESIRE

Your desire for personal growth is entirely aligned with an internal desire for manifestation that seeks to fulfill itself in one way or another, and only by working on it can you manifest it. The desire is there to propel you, to move you, to push you, to force you out of the "old you," and bring to light a new version of yourself.

Working with Desire

I once heard on a radio show in Argentina that what differentiates witches from wizards is that witches are individuals (men and women of any age) who were more focused on working magic simply to attract things, while the magicians were those individuals who were more focused on working not from learning, but from experience, in solving what was already done and thus achieving a life more based on personal success and wisdom than just having things.

I honestly think that they are not very different currents. Whether these are wizards, witches, or sorcerers, they all work with something very powerful–desire. The power of desire drives all in search of something better–the desire to be better, the desire to have a better house in a better location, the desire to have good friends who are with you all your life, the desire to love and be loved, the desire to help others evolve and grow, the desire to be more powerful or wise. These are all examples of the internal desire, for something that motivates us to get out of our comfort zone (probably the most uncomfortable area of all) to evolve, grow, and become better.

Where Does Desire Come From?

Desire arises from the absence of something. It is like an interior space that seeks to be filled in some way, similar to the sensation of appetite that can become hunger. That desire to eat leads you to look for food, but once the food is out of reach, the desire arises and becomes stronger and more powerful, as you become more anxious and more hungry for that need to feel satisfied. You no longer feel simply hungry, but starving, and that leads you to devour any plate of food within reach.

Desire first drives you to reason logically, and according to your knowledge and experience, that reasoning can motivate you to solve this problem. But if the problem is not solved as planned, the desire increases. From there, logic begins to fade, and little by little the desire feeds your anxiety for something (either physical or emotional) as you start looking for other less logical options to relieve that anxiety. And that is when despair arises.

The issue in the practice of sorcery is that many work from necessity, from despair, from a lack or absence of something, and when we work with rituals to attract that something, wishing to have it (love, money, health), we often do it from a feeling of emptiness. If your ritual receives this energy, what you are invoking can be confused, and the universe (those gods and angels of your personal belief) will end up giving you that emptiness back, instead of what you are wishing for.

The power of desire and the power to make wishes are so great that they can lead to despair when you feel that these wishes are not manifesting themselves properly in your life. That is why you must know what exactly you are wishing for—the purpose and the origin of this desire. So before you perform any ritual, take ten minutes to meditate on your desire, pay attention to your emotions and your thoughts, and properly align your intentions, attention, and emotions with that purpose. From there, from the certainty of what you are looking to fulfill and how fulfill it, you will know exactly what kind of ritual you need to perform.

What Happens after Desire?

Once we have a desire, whatever it may be, we have three immediate options that our mind puts into play to make us decide how high and necessary the fulfillment of this desire is for us.

First Option (The Optimistic Option)
Work to fulfill the desire.

If you want something strongly enough, it is best to go for it. So make it a priority. Then the desire grows into a dream, and once we take steps toward it, this desire/dream becomes a goal, then a project plan we seek to fulfill.

Second Option (The Pessimistic Option)
Deny this desire and assume that it is impossible.

If you refuse to seek the fulfillment of this desire, whatever the reason, it will always generate some general frustration, and frustration often leads us to feel worse about ourselves.

Third Option (The Conscious Option)
Analyze how strong this desire is and place it on your wish list.

This is where individuals with the most experience, maturity, and decision-making ability consciously assume that although a desire is not impossible, it may not be a priority. So they keep it in mind as something of a longer-term that can either happen or not, but that, for now, is not a priority.

Whichever one of these three main options you choose, desire will always achieve an end result: its fulfillment or abandonment.

When the wish is fulfilled, whatever your desire, you will embrace and appreciate it. But after that, the power of that desire ends. If you you want it to gradually improve or become something different, you will have to make a new wish, but once you have it, you simply stop wanting it.

When the wish is not fulfilled, it can lead to personal frustration, anxiety, and an endless stream of negative reactions, which, while not representing an absolute end to your attempts, can make you feel bad. We have probably all wanted something at some point that we did not get, and it is important to study those wishes from the past, identify the patterns among them, and review and study why they were not fulfilled. What was the obstacle in your process—lack of experience, lack of attempts, lack of support? Was it something to blame on your parents or their parenting model? Did you try and fail? Did you at least try?

I invite you to carry out that self-analysis so that you know exactly what is limiting and frustrating you. Once you can identify these patterns, you will know where to start when you want something new, what attitudes and thoughts to avoid, and what or who to lean on.

11

WISHES

Just as your dreams are powerful reminders that your unconscious put there to guide you, your wishes are there to nurture you every step of the way, to lead you to align yourself with your personal purpose, with that wonderful and magical someone that you are destined to be. Stop treating them as mere dreams and illusions; they are more powerful than you think.

The Magic in Wishes

From childhood we are told to make a wish. We spend our lives making wishes. We wish on stars, little coconuts, butterflies, fairies, temples, and lucky charms, but we forget to be aware of it and give the wish enough information about what we really want. It is not about asking; it is about knowing how to ask.

Once you make a wish (and you should do it more often), everything around you begins to work based on that wish. It is no coincidence that suddenly when you want something, signs for what you wished for begin to appear practically everywhere.

And the signs do not stop coming. The problem is that sometimes we decide to ignore them rather than obey them, either for fear that what we ask for will be fulfilled or for fear of becoming very seriously involved in a process that we may not want to be part of—like wanting a car but not those monthly payments; or wanting a baby, but once the signs begin to manifest, we think that perhaps we are not the parenting type; or wanting to go to college, but once it gets close to being fulfilled, we fear we may not succeed So we unconsciously choose to ignore those signals, leaving the whole process on indefinite pause.

Mirrors of Manifestation

The world is not as it is, the world is as we are . . .
And everything else you want, will end up manifesting itself
in the world around you.

Stars

Making wishes on a star is a habit that is so linked to our culture that many times we even do it unconsciously. We forget the fact that our universe is so magical and powerful that we are able to see gigantic balls of gas floating in the cosmos on the other side of the galaxy, entire planets, and complex planetary systems, like tiny points of light that open up the dark for us. All of this is so magnificent to our eyes that many prefer to ignore it, thus ignoring all the enormous power that is taking place in between.

Have you ever seen the stars? Probably yes, but do not doubt
then that the stars also saw you.

Making a wish on a star is as simple as closing our eyes for a moment, wanting what we want, visualizing in our mind what we want, then opening our eyes to ask the stars to fulfill that wish. The whole process is so simple, so subtle, that it makes us doubt its power of manifestation. After a while we stop believing in these desires, ignoring entirely that many of those we made years ago as children had already been fulfilled.

The power of the stars is not found on the surface of these distant, gigantic gas balls burning in the cosmos; their power is found in the connection that we have with them. It's our capacity as magicians that allows us to vibrate so high that we connect with the stars. And once we do, it is only a matter of time before our desires begin to manifest themselves.

Just as in magic we use candles to activate the power of a spell, fire, by nature, is the activator of energies (as is the color red). The stars live in the sacred space that surrounds us, burning and activating all the energy in the universe with their fire, like huge heavenly gods looking down to connect with and take care of us for our own good.

Once you make a wish on a star, your wish begins to travel long distances like a radio wave, which touches not one, but thousands and millions of stars at different times, and just like mirrors, each star sends that energy back once the wish has been activated on its fiery surface.

Djinns

We have created man out of clay, out of moldable clay

Before, from burning fire we had created djinns.

—Quran, 15, 26-27

At the dawn of humanity many gods emerged, many of them so ancient that they were older than our history. We are talking about an entire race of gods thousands, and perhaps tens of thousands, of years old.

Though these gods did not have names, they spoke the first languages of man, and their power was such that they transformed into all kinds of creatures and winged animals to sneak around among humans.

With the arrival of language and writing, the history and development of civilization, new gods came and inhabited our world. These new gods were venerated in the most diverse old religions, and with that, the old gods were ignored and considered something less than gods. So they dedicated themselves to inhabiting the deserts and older oceans that would have been abandoned by then.

Later, in the pre-Islamic world, the Arabs worshiped these old gods, or *djinn,* as supernatural beings of enormous power, but they were considered inferior to modern gods and thought of as demons of the desert or gods of the sands.

In Islamic mythology these dark desert gods would have been created from smokeless fire and could obey (as they had free will) the powerful Iblis God (the devil/deprived of all goodness).

While popular culture has turned djinns into more humorous creatures with possession of infinite power and bound to grant wishes, in myth these were beings of enormous power who were worshiped as gods and only granted wishes to their followers.

Djinns act as guardians of the temples and sacred places, granting wishes in exchange for gifts. In New Delhi, for example, there are temples dedicated to the djinn, where by tradition, tourists carry their wishes written on paper, along with many gifts, such as rose petals, exotic fragrances, flowers and perfumes, oils, and even food, in order to win their favor.

The sacred places in the world are many. Even today you could easily find a tattoo shop or a fast-food restaurant on what was once a sacred place. But the djinn continue to grant wishes to all those noble beings who give them gifts and some attention, even from a small altar.

Faeries

. . . And we can only make out their peculiar shapes mingling with our shadows, and we hear them whispering in the wind all kinds of old poems and proses, in so old languages we can vaguely distinguish from the natural sound of the wind.

Faeries have a power to captivate us that goes beyond our understanding, we have complete books, movies, series, comedies, and stories full of good faeries and dark faeries.

Faeries are immortal beings that inhabit our world but remain hidden from our eyes. They are living beings of nature that walk in our world from time to time, although they are easier to find in forests, rivers, lakes, and springs.

The world of faeries is quite complex; it is full of magical creatures beyond our imagination. There are even beings that do not appear in our books because they have never been seen. Whether represented as tiny forest creatures (pixies) or as powerful trail-keeping queens (faeries and sylphids), they are always associated with three things—the air element, the magic of granting wishes to good-hearted people, and femininity in nature.

Faeries use air as their home and also as their means of transportation. A typical Ecuadorian children's song says, "faeries build their little houses in the air, they are made of leaves and flowers and sway with the wind." They embody the feminine spirit of nature just as the fauns embody the masculine spirit; however, it is their facet as wish grantors that we love the most.

In the tropical jungle of Venezuela (essentially the Amazon), it is common to find gifts or amulets made with cinnamon sticks, orange wheels, and flowers, tied together with colored ribbons and hung from the branches of trees to win the favor of the *setas* and *forasi*, winged spirits of the forest of very short stature who transform into beautiful women to walk among men, granting wishes on full moon nights, but who also become angry women who punish traitors in the darkest nights when the moon is not seen in the sky.

Your magic does not come from any religion or any book, your magic comes from something much deeper and more ancient, it is that divine and inner connection with your ancestors, it is such an intimate connection that no one else can intervene in it.

12

RITUALS AND SPELLS

Look how far you've come,

In this book and in life.

Keep going . . . You're just getting started.

Twenty-One Rituals for Abundance and Wealth

In this book I have included twenty-one simple but powerful rituals to support your personal growth toward abundance, enrichment, and prosperity, all of them performed with much love and, most importantly, divine guidance.

These spells and rituals were elaborated and used by me at some point, from a wide list of spells in my grimoire. These

were chosen for one simple reason: they are the ones that have had the best results. They are the rituals that I always share with my readers, my followers, and my friends. Most of these rituals I know by heart, but that is not my goal for you. This book is a guide to spells and rituals dedicated to your personal growth, as well as to empower yourself like the powerful wizard and sorcerer that you are.

1. RITUAL WITH A MIRROR

A ritual that we keep active at home is the mirror of abundance. In addition to keeping large mirrors in practically all of our rooms, one of our mirrors has been consecrated as follows.

On the back of a full-length mirror I have drawn a pentacle (a five-pointed star) to energize the mirror. The mirror is then cleaned from bottom to top with a damp cloth using a mixture that combines water, with equal parts of musk, rosemary, verbena, and sandalwood oils, and then we wipe it again with a clean dry cloth.

The position of the mirror is important, so it is best to locate it where it reflects enough light, and if it can reflect the dining room table, it is a good way to double the abundant energy of the home.

Next to the mirror it is always good to place crystals, precious objects, and a bowl of plenty filled with rice, coins, and other grains.

2. CREATING AN IDOL OF ABUNDANCE

Next we are going to create a magical idol to channel the spirit of the home, then charge it with energy to transform it into a spirit guardian of abundance.

The Living Energies of the Place

All the places that surround us have been at some point in the past home to various other plants, animals, people, and spirits. The residual energies of these individuals continue to inhabit the place, and after some time they begin to become conscious, repeating the actions they see others perform.

Different cultures have found and studied these creatures to include them in their folklore. In Chinese culture these complex entities are called *Chimi* (entities that are formed from the air and the mist of the mountains) and *Moryo* (entities that are formed from the soul of rocks, mountains, and rivers). In Hawaii they are known as *Obake* (a term introduced there by the Japanese). In Latin America they are known as *Hadas* (not to be confused with faeries). In Afro-Caribbean culture they are known as *Ates,* and in Amazonia they are called *Babes.* All of these have the same characteristics and origin stories.

Once these energies group together and form one of these small entities, they do not stop growing and feeding on the remaining energy of all those individuals in the physical, astral, and spiritual environment, which is why having them as allies is an indispensable task—and extremely important.

The Realization and Consecration of the Totem

A totem or *skin* is a representative figure object of a spirit, divinity, or person that we use to communicate with the individual rrepresented. These totems not only serve to represent deities that we venerate, but they can also be used as skins for those lesser spirits who have difficulty interacting with us.

Although you can buy one in the market (there are many varieties), I recommend you make one yourself. My first totem was a representation of a spirit of nature that I made with modeling clay as a child, trying to do something similar to those elaborate ceramic and wooden figures that Mama always kept on the altar. I invite you to make it with the material of your choice and give it any shape you choose, which may well be a human, animal, or something else you associate with abundance.

Once you have purchased or made the totem, starting on a new moon day, place it in a pot or large bowl and fill it with soil from a nearby patio, garden, or park. Cover the totem entirely, and add some semi-precious gems and minerals to the ground to nourish it. I recommend quartz (energy channelers), amethyst (transmutation and protection), and agate (power development), but you can use other gems of your choice, even your birthstone.

Next add 1 ounce of verbena essential oil to the earth, light two white candles and a stick of mint incense, then recite the following enchantment three times.

Once upon a time there was a land and that land gave birth to its essence.

Once upon a time there was an essence, and that essence gave birth to many essences.

Once upon a time there were many essences together looking for a home.

Once upon a time there was a skin in the middle of the earth that saw them born.

Once upon a time there was a land that by decree is blessed.

Once upon a time there was a guardian spirit of great power that was born from this land.

Once upon a time there was a guardian spirit that was born from the many essences.

Once upon a time there was a guardian spirit that inhabited the home.

Once upon a time there was a spirit of abundance and protection born under my blessing.

Once upon a time there was a full moon night when this ritual was born.

Once upon a time there was tonight where the spirit that I consecrate and bless has decided to act for my good and will, and as long as it is, it will always be blessed in this home.

Next cover the earth with a towel and let the candles burn out completely. The next day light a white candle and another incense stick, repeat the spell, and so continue until the closest full moon night, which will be the last night.

When the last candle is consumed the night of the full moon, carefully extract the figure from the earth, clean it with a dry towel, and place it in a visible area of the home, preferably on your altar or a tall piece of furniture from which it can see the main room.

Maintenance

This totem has been impregnated by the energy of the earth, has been consecrated by the energy of the moon, and is inhabited by those spirits of conscious energy that inhabit the place. It is also a representation of your own abundance. You do not depend on it, but it does depend on you, and the better the relationship between you and it, the better the quality of your abundance. For that reason I advise you to take care of it. Give it a glass of water and change the water daily. From time to time you can offer water with honey, candles, incense, aromatic oils, and anything you think will help it.

Personal Practice

I maintain a small altar with several of these figures of abundance. Although the ritual can be complex, like everything in magic it requires perseverance and effort for it to have good results, so I invite you to try it. Personally, I write down the dates of the full moons corresponding to each one of my spirits of abundance so that I know how much time they have been with me, and as a traditional practice of my land, we place small dishes with candies, crystals, and aromatic oils near them.

3. THE SCROLL OF ABUNDANCE

This practice to focus your daily energy on a complex long-term goal (abundance, prosperity, and wealth in general) is to align your attention with your intentions of personal growth.

On a sunny day (avoid doing this on a rainy, overcast, or snowy day) early in the morning, light one green and one gold candle and a jasmine or amber incense stick. Grab a piece of parchment paper and pass it several times through the smoke of the incense. Next you will write the following words in capital letters on the parchment with gold ink: *abundance, prosperity, weatlth, good forutne, good luck, clarity, and money with good purpose.*

Once that is done, turn the paper over and draw, again with gold ink, a pyramid or triangle pointing upward, and in the center of the triangle draw the symbol of your country's currency, your full name, and the symbol of your zodiac sign. Next to the triangle you can draw two or three symbols that you personally consider positive and related to your energy, for example: a dollar symbol ($), arrows, stars, moons, pyramids, and so on . . .

Pass the parchment again through the incense smoke several times. Next anoint your hands with a few drops of essential oil of vetiver, sandalwood, or juniper. Then while keeping your eyes closed, anoint the paper on both sides with your hands, visualizing that the paper is high denomination banknotes and that the more you collect, the more they multiply. Take your time with this, it can be 3 minutes, 6 minutes, 15 minutes. Any amount of time that you think you will need to properly carry out this visualization.

Once you finish the visualization, recite this enchantment:

Oh great spirits who rule money and abundance

I (your full name) call you and ask you to listen to me.

Here I invite you to be part of my life and of this project.

To all of you good spirits of plenty and avatars of good fortune,

I invite you to express your good wishes on my growth path.

Here and now, I (your full name) call you and welcome you.

Just as desire is the wick that lights the fire of creation

so be your presence, the one that activates all prosperity,

abundance, and good fortune in a permanent and favorable way in my life.

That's right, that's how I decree it, and that's how I predict it.

Once you have finished reciting this enchantment, place the scroll you made with the anointed paper on your altar or in a tidy, visible space. Recite this enchantment for three days in a row, always after passing the parchment through the incense smoke. It can be at different times, depending on your availability. On the fourth day, after reciting the enchantment, burn the parchment in the flame of a golden candle and let it consume the paper completely.

This is not a spell, but rather a recommendation. The following symbol is a powerful emblem in its simplicity; it does not require anything elaborate that might confuse you or make you doubt, even for a second, the ritual you are performing.

I drew this symbol when I was eighteen years old when I started my job search. I had many options to choose from, and I was giving copies of my résumé to everyone. The problem was that I had not decided on any job, so I drew this emblem for a money ritual asking for guidance in 1) making the best decisions regarding the money I had; 2) choosing the best investments of my time and money (from which phone to buy to which house to live in); and 3) exploring which job to choose.

This emblem is simple to create and has only two functions. The first is to help you make the best decision for the long term when you have more than one option. Once it is complete, just follow the signs and your own intuition. The second is to protect your economic choices against the spells of someone else, for example, a sorcerer that is trying to negatively influence your employment or take the job that you want.

Below on the left is the original emblem that I drew to get my first job as a communications consultant, where I learned to interact directly with investors and sellers, as well as with the general public, and where

I gained experience (and contacts) to complement my college career in marketing and digital advertising, both tools that got me where I am today.

And next to the original emblem, is a second version that I drew years later, with more experience and practice. I recommend you use this circle to carry out your rituals related to money, investments, and good fortune. You will surely find throughout the book several rituals in which I suggest you draw this magic circle of wealth. If for some reason you do not have the time or the materials to do so, you can make a simple circle with a mixture of salt and rosemary (purification, protection, money).

5. BAR OF SOAP FOR MONEY AND WEALTH

This is a ritual intended for the most creative and entrepreneurial people, those who like to make things with their own hands. For years I have spent my free time making handmade soaps, both to have at home (thus avoiding chemical products that damage the environment) and to sell at craft fairs and in shops.

For years I have created many recipes, but this is the favorite of my friends, clients, and loved ones. For its realization you are going to need a large chunk of clear glycerin soap base and flexible, heat-resistant molds, gloves, and two cauldrons to use as a *bain-marie* or *double boiler*.

Oils
Choose two to three of these and apply 8 drops of each one to the mix.

- » Bay
- » Cinnamon
- » Honeysuckle
- » Myrrh
- » Neroli

- » Rosemary

- » Sandalwood

Herbs and Flowers
Choose between one and three of the following options, I recommend using ground, dried herbs and flowers, one tablespoon of each.

- » Bergamot root

- » Burdock

- » Eucalyptus

- » Laurel

- » Rose petals

- » Rue

Once you have all the ingredients together, boil the glycerin in the bain-marie. Once it melts to the proper consistency, add the oils and herbs, mix well, and very carefully (wearing gloves) pour the mix in the molds.

Make a circle with coarse salt and rosemary powder to remove any negative energy and strengthen the energy of money. In the center of the circle let the bars of soap cool for a few hours next to a gold or silver candle and a cone of sandalwood or rue incense.

After several hours or an entire night, unmold the soap and cover them with a dry cloth to preserve them. You can tie a green ribbon moistened with rue essential oil around each bar of soap. Remember to use it daily.

6. OIL TO ATTRACT MONEY AND GOOD FORTUNE

For the creation of this blend, I recommend using a glass bottle with a lid (no plastic bottles), and if possible, purchase the oils in the botanica or esoteric store of your choice.
You will need:

- » Two green candles and one gold

- » Rue incense

- » A tablespoon of dried sunflower petals

- » A tablespoon of dried yellow rose petals

- » ¼ rue essential oil

- » ¼ rosemary essential oil

- » ¼ neroli essential oil

- » ¼ sandalwood essential oil (If a spell is for money, sandalwood is probably included.)

Instructions:

The first thing you need to do is, on the night of the new moon, light a green candle and a rue incense stick to prepare the energy for the next morning. Then place the ingredients one by one in a bowl or cauldron, and mix them with a tablespoon made of wood or metal. Continue to stir them for several minutes in a clockwise direction to make sure the energy flows correctly.

The following morning, draw our magic circle of wealth in a suitable space, light the green and gold candles and an incense stick, and pour the oil very calmly and carefully into the glass bottle you have chosen. Seal the bottle completely and leave it there until sunset.

Store this blend in a place where it stays cool, and use it to consecrate talismans that attract money, bless rituals for prosperity, or add a few drops of this oil to the bathwater or the water you use to clean the house.

7. OIL SPRAY FOR HOME OR OFFICE

Once you have created your own *Oil to Attract Money and Good Fortune* from the above ritual, fill a glass jar that has a spray cap with the oil, a small quartz crystal to activate the energy, and a few drops of amber or ylang-ylang essential oil to balance the energy properly.

Label the bottle with a small personal decree so that every time you see it you decree it in your own head, such as: "This is the oil to attract wealth," "this is my personal blend that blesses all my corners with prosperity and economic abundance," "this oil is a magnet for money and wealth par excellence," or if it's for a business premises "this is my magic potion to attract good customers; they come here with a lot of money, find just what that they are looking for, and the aroma of this potion brings them back."

Make use of this blend of wealth by spraying every corner of your home, office, or workplace every morning, and if you would like, you can personalize it by adding two drops of your own perfume.

8. AROMATIC BATH TO ATTRACT GOOD FORTUNE

Here is an infusion to use with your bathwater (either in the shower or the tub). This bath can be done any day to attract good fortune and wealth.

If like me, you collect rainwater, water from nearby rivers, and waterfalls, I recommend using that for this ritual. If collecting the water is too difficult, you can use tap water that you have left undisturbed for at least one night.

Into a large cauldron add 32 fluid ounces (1 liter) of rainwater, followed by spoonfuls of each of the following herbs: dried ground bay leaf, couscous or catnip, dried sunflower petals, verbena, and vetiver. Mix the herbs well then add eight drops each of the following oils: eucalyptus, lavender or jasmine, and cinnamon, and close with a pinch of brown sugar.

Light some pine incense, a purple candle, and a green candle to properly transmute the surrounding energies to your own benefit, and let the mixture sit with these candles for about one half hour. At shower time you can accompany this bathwater with the *Bar of Soap for Money and Wealth* that we made previously or with a bar of coconut or olive soap.

9. BANQUET OF APPRECIATION TO DOUBLE YOUR ABUNDANCE

Once the child thanks their parents for something, even if it is something trivial or something material, they have a sense of fullness and tranquility that allows them to feel good, so seeking to repeat this feeling, the parents make an effort every time to feel the gratitude of their children more. Now remember, the universe and all its gods are in a way your parents too . . .

Nothing attracts more miracles than giving thanks. Once you are thankful, it is only a matter of time for the miracles to repeat. That is why I like to hold a gratitude banquet similar to a celebration party. I like to give thanks for every small opportunity, for every meeting, for every valid option to choose. I even like to give thanks for every obstacle that I have overcome, because each one of these obstacles has left me with a lesson.

For this ritual I recommend you prepare a good meal at home—dinner or lunch, either alone or with your loved ones (it is your decision). Serve it with a glass of water or wine and honey. Cover a golden candle with a few drops of lavender and ylang-ylang essential oil, light the candle, and use it to burn seven bay leaves (laurel is a natural energy protector and fire is a natural activator of energies). Place the candle in a spacious room, and celebrate your banquet.

Remember to make a toast, even if you are alone, to commemorate all your efforts, the lessons learned in the process, the decisions made, and the people you met in the process. Make the first one before starting the meal and another at the end.

This banquet is not only symbolic; it is a ritual of great power that I myself have performed in moments when I remember how much I have lived, how much I have overcome, and where I am and why.

This ritual works as a powerful decree. It is a statement that makes it clear that, regardless of the circumstances, you are worthy of where you are. Tell the universe or the deity of your personal pantheon that you are celebrating for it and looking forward to more reasons to celebrate.

10. MOJO BAG TO PROTECT THE ABUNDANCE OF THE HOME

On a new moon night, make a cloth bag as large as your clenched fist. Then draw our magic circle of wealth. Light a green candle and then

light some mint or strawberry incense.

Mix together equal parts benzoin powder, dried lily flowers, parsley, rosemary, lavender, mint leaves, and eucalyptus in a bowl. Use this aromatic mixture to fill the cloth bag, adding in a small piece of the golden thread with the herbs. Stitch the bag using a needle and thread to form a kind of sachet.

Place this amulet in the center of the ritual circle and light two silver candles. With your hands open palms upward you will recite the following enchantment:

Oh great spirits of good fortune, good trade, and money,

here I invoke you in this dark night to hear my spell,

here I call you who know abundance and prosperity,

and from here I call on you to heed my call and bless my ritual.

This amulet in your honor I consecrate, and so from this moment I decree

this talisman in all its names that I do not know, and I decree thus.

This tool of magic I present here before you to shower you with blessings.

So I decree and so I consecrate,

with your blessing this amulet will bring good prosperity to my home,

with your blessing this talisman will bring good fortune to this place.

Now, hold the amulet in both hands close to your heart and recite the enchantment a second time. Then take the amulet that has already been consecrated and assign it a place in the home, a place that will be yours and from which this amulet can take care of the financial security of your home.

11. THE SORCERESS BOTTLE FOR MONEY

Version I

- » 1 glass jar
- » 14 high-value coins
- » Honey
- » A bunch of rosemary
- » 1 white candle

Fill the jar by adding the coins one by one, and for each coin you add two teaspoons of honey. After placing all the coins, add the rosemary, light the candle, and seal the jar.

Shake the jar twice a day and light a candle next to the jar every Monday or Thursday morning.

Version II

- » 1 glass jar with a lid
- » 1 tablespoon of sesame seeds
- » 1 tablespoon of wheat flour
- » 1 tablespoon of brown sugar

» 1 tablespoon of corn kernels

» 12 coins of high or regular denomination

During the night of the full moon, fill the jar with all the elements, adding a personal element to the spell such as hair, nails, blood, saliva, or photos. Seal the jar, shake it with both hands very carefully, and then meditate and visualize your desires related to money with the jar in your hands. Repeat this meditation every week.

12. RITUAL TO DISPEL LACK, ANXIETY, AND CONFLICT AT HOME

This ritual complements an astrological symbol with magic to dissipate negative energy, which is why this ritual has clearer schedules than others.

You will perform this ritual between eleven p.m. Thursday night and one a.m. Friday morning. Thursdays are ruled by Jupiter, the planet of greatness and triumph, while Fridays are ruled by Venus, the planet that rules over all forms of love and appreciation, which will counter the energy that is usually promoted by Mars, the planet of conflict and war.

Starting at eleven p.m. you will draw a pentagram (a five-pointed star inside a circle) on the ground with chalk or paint. Make a second circle around the star with a mixture of salt and ground camphor. Light a black candle at each point of the star and burn a little sage to clean the energy of the place, for this you can use white sage in leaves or incense sticks.

In red or gold ink, write your full name and the address of the place, then draw a map of the inside of the home on a piece of paper. It does not have to be completely accurate, simply indicate the shape of the dwelling including the internal walls. On the back of the paper draw a star flanked by eight arrows, all these arrows pointing in different directions, as I specify in the drawing on page 147.

Inside the pentagram place your cauldron and fill it with equal parts of coarse salt, ground rosemary, white sage, rue leaves, and a

pinch of white pepper or powdered verbena root. Add eight drops of eucalyptus or mint essential oil, and mix it thoroughly with your hands.

Using a dagger, visualize the shape of a pentagram inside the cauldron, similar to the one you have drawn outside. Hold the dagger with both hands pointing toward the cauldron and recite:

With this enchantment I consecrate nature inside and below this place, with this enchantment I protect now and always the surroundings of this place.

Now, with the dagger in one hand pointing east and a handful of the enshrined herbs in the other, recite aloud:

As long as my magic is great and powerful I will watch over this place,

Just as my magic grows, the energy that protects this place will grow with me.

As long as my energy flows in this world, I will protect this and any place that I inhabit.

Just as my energy flows in this world, no evil can act within this place.

All bad omens lose power here, all entities and negative spectrum are removed from here.

everything that threatens the well-being of people in this place is removed far from here

Let it be it and so I (your full name) decree it.

Throw the handful of herbs in that direction, then following the same instructions make this decree in the other three directions. At the end, place the dagger in the circle next to the cauldron, place another handful of the herb mix in a saucer and burn it as incense. Join the rest of the mix with earth and plant in a nearby garden, this being your magic tribute to nature.

13. RITUAL TO INVOKE THE SPIRITS OF GOOD FORTUNE AND GENEROSITY AT HOME

For this ritual you will need a large, quiet space, preferably a room with a door to avoid distractions. You can also perform this ritual in a group, simply by adding the names of the other individuals you will perform with to the circle.

On a Sunday just before sunrise, draw a circle of salt, about six feet in diameter. Right in the center of the circle you will draw a symbol or figure of the sun (as simple or as decorated as you like). The sun will be flanked by various stars. Inside the circle you are going to write in the order of your preference the words *welcome, abundance, success, prosperity, wealth, well-being, health, love, joy,* your full name, the symbol of your zodiac sign, and the symbol of whichever monetary denomination you prefer.

Once the circle is complete, fill your cauldron with equal parts white sage and mint leaves (purification and protection), a handful of coarse salt (to nullify any negative intent in your subconscious), two pieces of white quartz (balance and power), a piece of pyrite (to focus and strengthen the mind), eight drops of lavender or patchouli oil (energy charge), a pinch of cinnamon powder (sweet thoughts), and a recent photograph of yourself.

Light a sage or eucalyptus incense stick and move the incense around the circle, both inside and outside. With your magic wand or dagger in hand (whichever you prefer) pointing upward as you walk around the circle, following the order, east, south, west, north, recite:

Oh great avatars who take care of the four cardinal points.

Oh great gods who rule in all four directions.

Oh great spirits that inhabit the four ways of this world.

To all those well-intentioned among you, I summon you at this time.

To all those with good wishes among you, I summon on this day of the sun.

To all those willing to help me among you, I call you at this time.

For each of the four directions I invoke you to come to me with all your treasures.

For each of these four routes I call you to come here and now with all your powers.

For each one of my good wishes that you can fulfill, here my light services I offer you.

May your acts of kindness act through me and may your light be the lamp in this world.

Come here to improve and bless everything you touch through my hands, come here where this humble sorcerer invokes you to dispel any misfortune and any disease.

Once you finish reciting the enchantment, light a yellow or gold candle, empty the cauldron completely on a piece of blue or purple fabric, and tie the ends of the fabric to form a sachet. Tie the sachet with a golden string and hold it in the center of the circle until the candle is completely consumed. This cloth bag is your *personal item of abundance,* which you can bury in the garden or keep hidden in a corner of the house away from the eyes of others, according to the spiritualist magic tradition. As long as you keep this bag with you, the spirits will continue to confer favors and well-being in exchange for being welcome to move in your space as long as there are no bad intentions in between.

14. THE CANDLE OF ABUNDANCE AND PROSPERITY

You will need:

- » A large wax or soy candle
- » Sandalwood, cinnamon, neroli, and orange essential oils, three drops of each
- » A dagger for drawing
- » A red or gold ribbon
- » Cinnamon powder and brown sugar
- » Some sprigs of cedar, peppermint, or pine
- » A cup filled with lentils and grains of rice
- » A mug filled with yellow or red rose petals
- » A cup filled with assorted seeds

On a full moon night, draw the magic circle, light a stick of cinnamon or mint incense, mix the oils and use them to anoint, dress, or moisten the candle. Cover the candle completely with cinnamon and sugar. Once the candle is properly anointed, write and draw on it (with the tip of the dagger or with a pin) your full name, five stars, and several arrows to raise energy.

Add a second layer of the oils and cinnamon to the candle, tie it with the ribbon making a total of eight knots. Place the candle on a saucer in the center of the circle, use the herbs, rice and lentils , petals, and seeds to fill the space around the candle, not as a decorative aspect, but to symbolize abundance and wealth.

Light the candle and recite the following enchantment:

May the wind change in my favor, may the avatars of well-being smile at me.

May the sacred fire of plenty make its way on my way.

May the sacred waters that enrich the field bless my path.

May luck and good fortune embrace me at all times and under all circumstances.

Let the candle burn until the end, then sweep and clean all the remains of the ritual, while you are cleaning, you must recite:

As abundance enters, deficiencies leave.

Just as prosperity embraces me, everything else goes away.

Just as I embrace everything new and good that is knocking on the door,

thus I scatter far from me and far from here, everything that has fulfilled its function.

Repeat this ritual for at least three full moons in a row.

15. THE RITUAL CIRCLE OF PROSPERITY

The circle of prosperity is a metaphysical concept that seeks to focus the energy of money and wealth on a single point, and from there, spread it throughout the environment. That point is your home or room, and from there the energy you produce will begin to move toward the rest of your environment.

To carry out this ritual you will need:

» A spacious, quiet space, it can be on a table or on the floor

» Colored chalks, aromatic salts, or dry herbs

- » Incense of myrrh and sandalwood
- » A plate containing different gems, crystals, and minerals
- » A saucer of dried flowers
- » A dish of aromatic herbal oil
- » A censer
- » A staff
- » Candles of different colors and sizes
- » A white candle with a human shape to symbolize you
- » A recent photograph

As if you were creating an altar, you should choose a space to carry out this circle. I advise you to do it on a table, but you can also do it on the floor in the house. In the chosen space, burn some myrrh and sandalwood incense for purification purposes, then draw a circle of about three feet diameter in that space using colored chalk, aromatic salts, or a mixture of herbs and dried flowers to symbolize the abundance of nature.

Once the circle has been made, place within it a plate with crystals, rocks, and quartz of different colors, a plate with herbs and fresh flowers of your choice, a plate with oil of aromatic herbs (can be rosemary, sage, eucalyptus, mint, or cedar), a censer, candles of different sizes and colors (at least three), a glass of water, a pentagram (can be drawn on paper), the white candle with a human shape to represent yourself, and the symbol that you see below.

The more prosperous and abundant your circle looks, the more powerful this ritual will be, because abundance is represented by the elements chosen by you personally (symbolizing your decisions) and by their practicality. Nothing here is decorative, nothing belongs to others, and nothing is missing. Each element present in this ritual has a function to attract, channel, or energize something else that comes from outside, for your own convenience and benefit.

Next you will take five minutes to meditate in front and outside of your circle. Contemplate your work in complete silence, take a deep breath, and meditate, visualizing each of the items in front of you. You will then meditate out loud decreeing the reason why each of these items is present in the circle following this structure:

These herbs will attract money and wealth so that I never lack anything.

These flowers symbolize nature so I don't lack balance in my life.

These aromatic oils nourish to feed my soul and my home.

These lights (candles) so there is always clarity and light along my way.

This incense to honor my home and everyone who lives in it.

Like so, you will identify the function of each item therein, decreeing your power over each item, and its function, thus making clear what work is to be done. After the meditation, I invite you to light the incense of your choice in the censer, and also the candles, and stand in front of the altar with your arms open to recite the following enchantment out loud:

I embrace with love everything that comes my way for my own convenience.

I embrace with devotion everything that (name of your personal deity) wants to give me.

I embrace from the heart all the good that comes to me and that is present in my life.

I let go from this moment all lack, all fear of success, and every prejudice that I have.

I embrace from today the abundance that has always been present and I have mistakenly ignored many times.

I embrace every blessing placed in my path, and I hold tight to all those blessings and positive changes that are coming into my life for my own convenience.

Once you have recited this as many times as you want or need to, the ritual is basically over. It is only a matter of letting the candles and incense completely consume themselves, then picking everything up. But I also invite you to play with your creativity. You can read a poem or write some inspired verses under the energy of this ritual and dedicate those verses to your loved ones or (why not?) to yourself. You can also serve a glass of wine to celebrate in communion with the spirits that this ritual has been performed.

16. RITUAL OF GRATITUDE TO INCREASE PROSPERITY

What is Gratitude?

If desire is that force that drives us from within to continue to pursue our dreams and goals, and instinct and experience are those forces that guide us in decision-making, it is gratitude that concretizes the goals achieved and appreciation that pure and magical ritual through which we say to the universe (and your personal god), "Thank you, thank you for the wishes granted, thank you for the motivation, and thank you for making concrete what I wanted."

Thankfulness is the way we say to a force greater than ourselves, "You gave me exactly what I wanted or needed, and I am grateful for it." It is a way of making this force that is superior to us, aware that we appreciate its work and hope it will continue. Otherwise, if we do not thank for what has been received or accomplished, the energy stops favoring us, stops working for our benefit, and life gets more complicated.

That is why for many years I have personally performed many small rituals of thanksgiving and, much more importantly, acts of gratitude, because the act of giving thanks is the sacred path through which we multiply the miracles and experiences that have occurred in our lives.

The Meditation

To begin this ritual, first write down all your wishes that have been fulfilled and everything you remember ever wishing for. If it is difficult for you to remember, try to recall where you were ten years ago and what you were doing or planning, then think about where you are now. Think about the people, places, rituals, traditions, moments, and experiences you have known. From there, take whatever time you need to meditate on it.

Next light an apple or cinnamon incense stick to let the thoughts of gratitude flow and read the entire list out loud. It doesn't matter if you cry, or smile, or appreciate some of these things—at some point they were obstacles that became valuable to you. Now dedicate yourself to thanks, and let the emotions flow like the energy you put into them as you recite the following:

Thank you universe, thank you for all these wishes that have been manifested, thank you for all these acts of your divine goodness, I, (your full name), I thank you from the bottom of my heart, today and always.

At the end burn the paper with the flame of a blue candle starting from the corners to the center.

17. SECOND RITUAL OF GRATITUDE

You will need:

- » Colored chalks, aromatic salts, or a bunch of dried herbs
- » Candles (red, green, and blue)
- » Patchouli or sandalwood essential oil
- » A pin
- » A censer and incense for Jupiter (roses or frankincense)
- » A glass of water and honey

- » Yellow flowers

- » A piece of amber

- » Two glasses of white wine

With colored chalk, aromatic salts, or a combination of dry herbs, draw a circle on the floor, and inside the circle a triangle. I like to do it with a large bunch of dry rosebuds, which you can buy at a nearby botanica. Now apply a few drops of oil on your hands and cover the candles from top to bottom with the oil, draw a triangle pointing upward on each of the candles with the pin, and place each of these three candles at each point of the triangle.

In the center of the ritual triangle place a blue candle, the glass of water and honey, the censer, a sunflower, a bunch of daisies or yellow roses, and a piece of amber. Light the incense and the candles from the outside in, and recite the following enchantment:

From the inside out I show how grateful I am for everything granted, and from the outside in, I open all my cycles (personal, professional, and magical) to say thanks to the universe for each one of these, and for the progress I have experienced.

From the outside in, the universe comes with all kinds of gifts for me, and from the inside out, my inner universe connects with all these gifts, gifts and blessings that I appreciate—open doors that bring me closer to what I seek, and closed doors that they take me away from everything that does not suit me.

With open arms I dedicate myself to thanks for all the favors granted, and with open arms I receive all the favors and gifts for my well-being that are on the way.

So be it, and so mote it be.

Once you have finished reciting the above, place a glass of white wine inside the triangle and hold the other with your left hand. Raise the glass before you at eye level and recite aloud:

With you who have granted me all the good, with you I toast to all our successes big and small, Thank you.

Next slowly drink the glass of wine, as you meditate on everything for which you are grateful. You can do it while reading a book or listening to music. When the candles are completely consumed, place the flowers, glasses, crystals, and everything corresponding to the ritual on your altar. After two nights you can clean the glasses and keep one of them filled with water on your altar, remove everything else. You can change the flowers for new ones if you prefer.

18. PERLA DE LA FORTUNA (A FORTUNE PEARL)

Do you have an old pearl necklace from your grandmother or your mother that you do not wear or use, but don't want to get rid of either? Why not let it serve as a magical tool to attract money, abundance, and wealth?

To welcome good fortune into your home, draw a small circle with white chalk on the floor. Inside the circle draw a triangle or a pyramid and inside that, light three white candles anointed with lavender or lilac essential oil. In the center of the circle, place a real pearl or a crystalline quartz cut like a pearl (do not use plastic pearls).

Light some incense, preferably with the same aroma of the oil you used for the candles. Remember that the function of the incense is to cleanse and change the energy of the air, while the oil in the candles is to enhance the type of energy you are conjuring. The pearl is in this case the battery that you are charging with this energy that you are transforming and channeling.

Once the candles have been consumed, collect the pearl and place it in the center of a saucer in a high place in the house, room, or apartment where it will receive light, making this pearl a portal to the light through which the energy of your home will always be attracting prosperity.

Note: If you wish, you can also perform this same spell on an entire pearl necklace and wear it from time to time. When you are not using it, keep it in a lit place, never in the dark.

19. TURN YOUR WALLET INTO A MONEY MAGNET

You will need the highest denomination bill you can get in your local currency.

On a crescent moon night, light a sandalwood, tangerine, or myrrh incense cone and a green candle (if you want to do well in a new business) or golden candle (if you want to attract good fortune and money).

Empty your wallet, then rub a few drops of frankincense essential oil and myrrh into your hands, and hold the wallet with both hands as you recite:

Thanks to my good creative and transmuting energy, nothing is ever missing here, this space is ready and prepared to be filled with riches, with abundance, with a rich and abundant prosperity.

Run your wallet through the incense smoke several times clockwise. Open and close the wallet several times visualizing with your mind's eye how it fills up, and keep in mind that every time you open it, it is to put money in it. Do not think about debts, do not think about past payments, visualize the abundance that will allow you to cover everything you may or may not need.

Now put inside your wallet: Your personal identification, the bill, or bills, several coins of different denominations in your local currency, and three dry bay leaves. While you are doing this recite:

Here begins to enter what I have requested, and less than this will not enter, because so I decree it, and so it is, and so it will be.

Then put the rest of your belongings back in the wallet.

20. INCENSE TO WARD OFF LACK AND ATTRACT WEALTH

In the morning, light a white candle (purification), a green candle (riches), and a red candle (to activate the energy of money), then combine the following dry plants in a cauldron: garlic skin, rosemary, sage, peppermint, bay leaf, star anise, orange peel, and frankincense. Add nine drops of good fortune essential oil—this may be our *Oil to Attract Money and Good Fortune* recipe or another oil of your choice. As you add the oil, recite:

Each drop of this oil that I consecrate in my hands is a step that cleans this space and lets in wealth and lets in abundance.

Burn the mixture in the cauldron and let the smoke from this incense flood every corner of the place.

21. CONSECRATE A SOCIETY WITH GOOD UNDERSTANDING AND ABUNDANCE

If you are participating in a society, a group of entrepreneurs, or are having problems with your partners, I suggest you carry out this ritual for three nights in a row.

On a Thursday night, draw our magic circle of prosperity, burn a combination of sage and rosemary in a saucer to clean the energy of the place, and light a purple candle for transmutation and progress.

In the light of this candle use a pin, your dagger, or athame to write the name of the company, society, or enterprise on a golden candle and the names of all associated individuals (including you) on green candles.

At the top of each candle, draw a small pentagram flanked by two arrows pointing upward, one on each side. Dampen the candles with lemon and myrrh essential oil.

Tie these candles together with a green or white ribbon and recite:

This society progresses as a team,

each member, each mind, we are all clear about our goal.

Our intentions are clear and our purpose is clear.

With each step of each we all progress.

May wealth and mutual understanding be our goal,

that abundance and eloquence are present in every thought,

that progress and nobility are present in every act.

Light the green candles first, burn some crushed and dried bay leaf in their flames, and then light the golden candle while reciting:

Sweet society, sweet progress

blessed be you at all times

May wealth accompany your name

and may good fame flank your path.

During the following two nights, light a golden candle in the same part of the ritual, to continue with the exercise of manifestation, to strengthen and consolidate the energy of this ritual, and to convince those spirits and deities that assist us, that we are taking this ritual seriously.

A Little Magical Gift Just for You

As you manifest abundance in your life, you connect with the purpose of your existence and incarnation. You connect with that good and that light that is destined to find you and embrace you.

Be aware of what you are expressing:

Why?

What for?

Where does it come from?

From what emotion?

From what need?

From what circumstance?

Manifest consciously.

This book of abundance came to your hands with twenty-one powerful rituals to improve your life. But my greatest wish is to empower you, so here I give you eight different little rituals to complement your magical recipe book, hoping each of them will work with you to usher in a different phase of your life.

MOON OIL BLEND

A simple blend that you can make on a Monday at any time of the day to anoint your candles with moon energy. Mix equal parts of essential oils of lily, lilac, violet, and chrysanthemum. Store this blend of essential oils in a glass bottle or jar and keep it on the window all night long, Pick it up at dawn, and store it in a cool, dark place.

Make use of this aromatic blend to anoint candles that you will use in your rituals whenever you want to attract extra lunar energy.

SIMPLE RITUAL TO LET GO OF SADNESS

Emotions are part of our process as human beings, they are part of us, and all emotions fulfill some function in us. But sometimes a negative emotion, especially sadness, can prevent us from moving forward if we do not handle it properly. A negative emotion that gets out of control can drag us into a very serious depressive cycle and make us forget about all the other good experiences that life offers us. That is why in magic you will find different methods to deal with these situations, but by helping you to heal properly and let go of that sadness without suppressing the emotion in any way.

I have personally performed this simple ritual on several occasions and have recommended it to many of my friends and loved ones when they are dealing with strong emotional reactions. It is extremely simple, and, after a couple of nights of sleep, you will begin to notice its effects.

It consists of taking a white rose with a long stem, anointing a white cloth ribbon with myrrh and lilac oil, and winding the ribbon over the entire stem of the rose and tying a knot at the end, revealing only the rose and its petals. This symbolically ties, not the emotions as such, but their influence and helps you take control of them.

Once that's done, sit at the edge of a nearby river with the rose, and recite those regrets that you want to let go of. Next hold the rose high over your head for a few moments in complete silence and, with eyes closed, visualize those sorrows and sadness that cause you pain while you focus on the sound of the river. Then throw the wrapped rose into the river and let it go. Those ailments will float away with the rose, and, after a few weeks, you will notice the difference.

CLEANSING THE SUBCONSCIOUS

If you feel that something is bothering your subconscious—a doubt or a memory of past events that won't stop coming to mind, the memory of a traumatic situation that you have lived through, or a nightmare that has been haunting your recent nights—hold two black candles in your hands, close your eyes, relax, take a deep breath, and think about the matters in your head that you want to reveal.

After a few minutes thinking about it, light the two candles and an orchid-scented incense. Focus your gaze for a few minutes on the candle flame and the scent of incense. This ritual will help you to illuminate and reveal little by little what inhabits your subconscious that is causing you discomfort. Once the situation is revealed, you will know what exactly you are dealing with, and you can then focus on finding the correct way to solve it.

COMBAT NIGHTMARES AND MENTAL BLOCKS

One of the simplest methods for this consists of taking a white candle with one hand and passing it several times around an individual's head while they remain calm with their eyes closed. That night light the candle, and it will consume all evil associated with the mind of that person.

A more modern and effective version consists of practicing the same operation, but in this case with a black candle previously anointed with a mixture of orange and eucalyptus oils, for its purifying qualities, then lighting the candle in a corner next to a clean water glass. In the morning collect the remains of the ritual and pour the water out of the house, repeating this little ritual three nights in a row.

TO ANNUL MAGIC JOBS AND PSYCHIC ATTACKS

A ritual for this consists of writing your full name, or the name of the person in question, next to a white candle and a black candle and lighting them together on a waning moon night, in order to diminish the power of any spell or hex while cleaning the energy simultaneously.

MOON CHARM BAG

To encourage your own creativity, imagination, and development of individuality—especially for artists, advertisers, and entrepreneurs—on a Monday night, light a white candle and an opium incense stick, and proceed to fill a white or silver cloth bag with dried white rose petals, complemented by a quartz crystal, and a silver coin or a piece of aquamarine.

Consecrate this magic pouch on the altar with a few drops of lilac or violet essential oil.

HEALTH CHARM BAG

To protect your body, especially the nervous and lymphatic system, and fight depression and feelings of loneliness, we will make use of Saturn's energy.

Let an orchid dry in the sun. Once it has completely dried, pulverize it until it is as close to dust as possible and store it until the indicated day. On a Saturday between evening and dusk, light one black and one brown candle, a copal or sage incense stick, and fill a black cloth bag with the orchid powder and a piece of coral.

Consecrate and activate the energy of this magic bag with a few drops of copal or sage incense and keep it stored somewhere in the bedroom.

NULLIFY A HEX OR SPELL

When a hex has been carried out, there are two very difficult things you must do. The first is to differentiate the effects of the hex—headaches, insomnia, tiredness, depression, bad luck, and so forth—from the common events of the day, and the second is to end the curse, because once the energy has begun to move in one direction seeking to affect someone, reversing it takes serious and complex work. As a curse takes its time to take effect, it settles into the life of the haunted, delving into every aspect before acting. Once it is activated, the hex is quite advanced.

Reversing curses can take weeks to complete and requires the help of experts in the field, since someone must be able to distinguish the exact effects of the curse, where it came from, and how it was carried out. It must also be someone trustworthy and who has enough power to combat an energy that has been moving against someone for a long time and send it back. It is as difficult for a magician as entering a river and trying to return the water to its origin.

Overriding a curse is in some ways an easier task, though it also requires some experience and preparation, but in the end it is easier to build a dam than to return the river water to its source.

The first thing you should do is wash several small, preferably circular, mirrors with a mixture of rosemary oil and water, properly polish them with a clean, dry handkerchief, and place them near the door, since mirrors have the magical quality of returning bad wishes back to their origin. This will only return that energy that arrives from that moment on, not the energy that already entered.

Next make a circle on the floor with a mixture of coarse salt and rosemary, and inside it draw the symbol of the sacred star of King Magician Solomon, which consists of two superimposed squares, one on top of the other, forming an eight-pointed star. This sacred symbol rejects evil and drives it away in all directions. To activate the magic of the circle you must place a white candle on each of its points and a ninth candle in its center, light them in an order starting from the northeast to the south, and continue north to move the energy properly and transform it in your favor.

This ritual must be complemented with a prayer to the spirit of the place where the ritual is performed, so this benevolent spirit will send away all evil. Because this prayer must be from the heart, don't write anything for it. Instead when the time has come, from inside the circle, sitting or standing next to the ninth candle, imploring the local spirit to gather all the present and future effects of this hex and send them back to their origin and to send that origin so far away they will never return.

Once the ritual is carried out and the last candle is consumed, leave the circle and clean space where the ritual was carried out, using a large bucket filled with water and aromatic oils, then burning a little myrrh or sage to calm the remaining energies in the place.

Prayers

Be aware of what you think

Be aware of what you say

Be aware of what you do

Be aware of what you learn

Be aware of what you teach

Be aware of what you repeat

Be aware of what you manifest.

Be aware, be conscious of your mind.

Daily Prayer of Abundance to the Great Spirit

Oh great spirit of the divine abundance that you rule and inhabit in all good things,

Divine sacred presence of abundance and wealth in every moment of our lives,

Welcome here where I implore you, in my heart and in my mind and in all my experiences,

Consecrate my life and each of my steps with your divine prosperity and infinite blessings,

Make me understand and recognize those mistakes I have made against my own benefit

Wrap me in your halo of divine protection, wealth, and joy,

And make me a light for all those who seek abundance in their lives.

I beg you to send your sacred light that multiplies in my life everything that benefits me.

I call you to live in each of my actions and thoughts,

and that your presence in my life is reflected in the achievement of all my endeavors.

I ask you to help me make the most convenient decisions for myself

and that once I reach all my goals,

I have the power to attract others like me along the path of wealth,

abundance, and prosperity, today and forever,

So mote it be!

Daily Prayer to the God of Abundance Who Rules the East

O great god of abundance that you multiply everything and that you reflect everything,

You who live in the East of the Cosmos,

I invoke you and call upon you to make yourself present in each of my acts.

May your divine presence be what drives this and every moment of my life,

that all the good and only the good multiply now and always,

and that you remove from my path everything that steals my energy and does not let my processes flow.

So mote it be!

Daily Prayer to the Spirit of Prosperity that Rules the West

Oh great spirit of prosperity that everything you touch prospers and grows,

you who dwell in the West of all that has been created,

I call you and ask you to bless with your presence all my projects and endeavors.

I pray in your name that prosperity is not absent.

I decree in your name, oh great spirit, that you promote prosperity.

I order the universe to remove in your name any aspect of lack in my life.

So mote it be!

Daily Prayer to the King of all Wealth that Governs the North

O great king that knows and keeps all the riches of the world,

you are the first and the last of all the great kings,

ancestral spirit that inhabits in the North of the created Cosmos,

May your wisdom guide my decisions on the road closest to your glory,

May your hand guide the direction of my steps on the road to success,

May your strength to find treasures and safeguard riches embrace me,

and may your ancestral presence be the force that drives my steps.

So mote it be!

Daily Prayer to the Golden Lion of Good Fortune that Rules the South

Oh great golden lion of good fortune, luck, and prosperity,

sacred creature that protects the dream secrets and the riches of heaven,

powerful and wise beast that illuminates with your presence the path to riches,

May you be, king of ancient kings and servant of the old gods,

the one that accompanies me at every step and on every path,

you who protect the South of the Cosmos and inhabit its frontiers,

you who between kings and emperors have dwelled,

elevate my presence in this life, guide me and protect me in the right direction

take me away from misfortune, disease, and lack,

bless me with good fortune, prosperity, and luck today and always.

So mote it be!

Appendices

Many of your energy blocks come from outside, and many come from within.

But the blocks are never superior to you, they are the same size,

once you learn where that energy block comes from,

then you are greater than the block and you are able to overcome it.

Energetic blockages have a negative effect on various aspects of your life.

Blocking love, abundance, your power of manifestation, health, joy, the projects you do, your creativity, your learning process, or your ability to enjoy daily pleasures.

Three More Money Spells

NEW YEAR'S EVE HOODOO MONEY SPELL

A gift from Miss Aida, author of *Hoodoo Cleansing and Protection Magic: Banish Negative Energy and Ward Off Unpleasant People*.

- »   12 grapes (to represent each month of the year)
- »   Alfalfa, fumitory herb, or both (money drawing herbs)
- »   A handful of washed quarters and dimes
- »   A bathtub filled with water (comfortable temperature)

Boil about 16 ounces of water. Once the water boils, remove the pot from the stove and add your herbs. Let the herbs steep in the water for 5 minutes. Strain the herbs (but keep the herbs) and add the water to the bathtub along with the coins. Ten minutes before midnight, pray Psalm 23 aloud and ask God to bring you a year filled with money. Remain in the bathtub and, at 2 minutes before midnight, eat one grape at a time while stating aloud that money will come to you each month of the year. You may exit the bathtub anytime after midnight. The following day dry off the money. Put the coins along with your picture in a small jar and bury it in your front yard. Place the herbs outside your front door.

PSALM 23

[1] The LORD is my shepherd; I shall not want.

[2] He maketh me to lie down in green pastures: he leadeth me beside the still waters.

[3] He restoreth my soul: he leadeth me in the paths of righteousness for his name's sake.

[4] Yea, though I walk through the valley of the shadow of death, I will fear no evil: for thou art with me; thy rod and thy staff they comfort me.

[5] Thou preparest a table before me in the presence of mine enemies: thou anointest my head with oil; my cup runneth over.

[6] Surely goodness and mercy shall follow me all the days of my life; and I will dwell in the house of the LORD for ever.

FAST MONEY ABUNDANCE CHARM BRACELET

You need:

» Star anise seed

» Allspice berries

» Cinnamon sticks

» Cloves

» Nutmeg/jayfal

- »   Bay leaves

- »   Dried lemon slices

On a night between the crescent moon and full moon, tie all the elements together with a braid of red, gold, and green, or white yarn. Keep it close and use it in the left hand.

TAROT MONEY SPELL

You need:

- »   A Wheel of Fortune tarot card

- »   A bowl filled with white rice and uncooked corn kernels

- »   Two gold candles

- »   Myrrh incense

Fill the bowl with white rice at the bottom, and add a layer of corn on it, place the Wheel of Fortune tarot card in the bowl facing up, light the candles and incense and place them around the bowl. Recite three times: "May the destiny be willing to change his signs, may good fortune smile on me, may good luck embrace me, may the coming changes be positive."

Recommended Titles

Although not all the books in this list are entirely related to the work of this book, each one has inspired this work in one way or another, or they are written by an author who inspired me in some way while I was writing this book.

- »   *A Kitchen Witch's Guide to Recipes for Love & Romance: Loving You * Attracting Love * Rekindling the Flames.* Dawn Aurora Hunt (Tiller Press, 2020).

» *The Alchemy of Inner Work: A Guide for Turning Illness and Suffering Into True Health and Well-Being.* Benjamin Fox and Lorie Eve Dechar (Weiser Books 2020).

» *The Big Book of Practical Spells: Everyday Magic That Works.* Judika Illes (Weiser Books 2016).

» *The Book of Candle Magic: Candle Spell Secrets to Change Your Life.* Madame Pamita (Llewellyn 2020).

» *Charms, Spells, and Formulas.* Ray T. Malbrough (Llewellyn 1986).

» *City Magick: Spells, Rituals, and Symbols for the Urban Witch.* Christopher Penczak (Weiser Books 2012).

» *The Complete Book of Moon Spells: Rituals, Practices, and Potions for Abundance.* Michael Herkes (Rockridge Press 2020).

» *Crystal Basics: The Energetic, Healing, and Spiritual Power of 200 Gemstones.* Nicholas Pearson (Destiny Books 2020).

» *Good Juju: Mojos, Rites & Practices for the Magical Soul.* Najah Lightfoot (Llewellyn 2020).

» *Hoodoo Cleansing and Protection Magic: Banish Negative Energy and Ward Off Unpleasant People.* Miss Aida (Weiser Books 2020).

» *Horse Magick: Spells and Rituals for Self-Empowerment, Protection, and Prosperity.* Lawren Leo and Domenic Leo (Weiser Books 2020).

» *Intuitive Witchcraft: How to Use Intuition to Elevate Your Craft.* Astrea Taylor (Llewellyn 2020).

» *The Little Book of Saturn: Astrological Gifts, Challenges, and Returns.* Aliza Einhorn (Weiser Books 2018).

» *The Little Work: Magic to Transform Your Everyday Life.* Durgadas Allon Duriel (Llewellyn 2020).

» *Lunar Alchemy: Everyday Moon Magic to Transform Your Life.* Shaheen Miro (Weiser Books 2020).

» *Madame Pamita's Magical Tarot: Using the Cards to Make Your Dreams Come True.* Madame Pamita (Weiser Books 2018).

» *Modern Witch: Spells, Recipes & Workings.* Devin Hunter (Llewellyn 2020).

» *Mountain Conjure and Southern Root Work.* Orion Foxwood (Weiser Books 2021).

» *Orishas, Goddesses, and Voodoo Queens: The Divine Feminine in the African Religious Traditions.* Lilith Dorsey (Weiser Books 2020).

» *The 21 Divisions: Mysteries and Magic of Dominican Voodoo.* Papa Hector/Hector Salva (Weiser Books 2020).

» *The Witch's Mirror: The Craft, Lore & Magick of the Looking Glass.* Mickie Mueller (Llewellyn 2016).

Closing Words

Because where this book is, where this book is kept, where this book rests, we are all blessed, we are all abundant, we are all prosperous, and we all enjoy health, wealth, good fortune, and well-being.

So mote it be!

ACKNOWLEDGMENTS

Thank you Miss Aida, Judika Illes, and Madame Pamita for your inspiration. Thank you, Dave, for everything, and each one of my readers, clients, and friends, for you patience and incredible support.

ABOUT THE AUTHOR

Born in Venezuela to a family of spiritual and magical healers, Elhoim Leafar lives in New York City, where he is manifesting his best life. A shaman, diviner, and magician who is influenced by traditional Afro-Caribbean mythology, he teaches throughout New York City, making annual appearances at WitchsFest and New York Pagan Pride. Find him at *elhoimleafar.com* and follow him on Instagram (@ElhoimLeafar).